TWELVE LIES
YOU HEAR ABOUT
THE *Holy Spirit*

Tim Riter

D1427941

NE✚GEN®

Building the New Generation of Believers

An Imprint of Cook Communications Ministries
COLORADO SPRINGS, COLORADO • PARIS, ONTARIO
KINGSWAY COMMUNICATIONS, LTD., EASTBOURNE, ENGLAND

NexGen® is an imprint of
Cook Communications Ministries, Colorado Springs, CO 80918
Cook Communications, Paris, Ontario
Kingsway Communications, Eastbourne, England

TWELVE LIES YOU HEAR ABOUT THE HOLY SPIRIT
© 2004 by TIM RITER

www.timriter.com

First Printing, 2004
Printed in the United States of America
1 2 3 4 5 6 7 8 9 Printing/Year 08 07 06 05 04

Cover Design : BMB Design/Scott Johnson

ISBN: 0-78144-057-2

At the risk of seeming simplistic, I would like to dedicate this book to the Holy Spirit.

He has simultaneously gently and firmly wooed me; he has taught and guided me; he has convicted and empowered me; he has drawn me to himself even as I ran from him.

Any mistakes in this book or in my life are my soul responsibility, not his. They express my failure to allow him to fill me.

Thank you, Spirit. May I continue to learn to walk with you.

Contents

Introduction

We Need a Supernatural Touch

So I say, live by the Spirit.
—Paul the apostle, in Galatians 5:16

Why do some Christians seem to have no gusto in their faith? They attend church services, they serve the Lord and others, they give of their time and their material possessions, but they never seem to burn with passion for God. They don't dig deep into him. They have a genuine faith, and they love God, but they clearly miss something in their spiritual lives.

Other Christians are different. They have no more talent or intelligence, but their lives have a spiritual zest. Passion motivates their actions. They would never claim to be sinless, yet sin seems to become less and less frequent among them.

What's the difference? The key to the dynamic Christian life is being filled with the Spirit, a concept I once thought would never apply to me. After all, I wasn't a charismatic, and I knew just what to do to be a good Christian. If I just did my best, I reasoned, God would be pleased when I stood at heaven's gate. I never suspected that my faith would later self-destruct.

As a child and young adult, I excelled at doing what everyone said a Christian should do: "Be regular in church and Sunday school," and I rarely missed, unless I was sick. "Give 10 percent to the church," and I tithed my allowance and money from odd jobs. "Be a virgin," and with great difficulty I remained one. "Don't drink and get drunk," and although I sneaked a sip of

9

my Dad's beer on occasion, I only experienced drunkenness while watching it in my friends.

Then came the ultimate sacrifice for God. At a high school church camp before my senior year, the speaker encouraged us to make a decision: either to enter a saving relationship with Christ or to enter full-time Christian service. I'd already done the first, so after numerous verses of "Just As I Am," I walked down to join many of my friends at the front. I would be a missionary to Africa. I wanted to "do the right thing." I also wanted what I thought would be a guaranteed ticket to heaven.

I did it all, and as well as anyone could expect. So why did my faith fall apart? After just one year at a Christian college to prepare for the ministry, my faith dissolved—not from moral decay, nor from doubts about God's existence. I merely realized I had no significant faith.

I did "what I was told," but faith was never deeply mine. I focused on surface behavior, behavior that never satisfied the deep yearnings for God, for purpose, for something to be passionate about spiritually.

Four years of painful searching revealed the key: being filled with the Spirit. This did not mean speaking in tongues or exercising any of the other charismatic gifts, but moving beyond surface behavior to a deeper relationship with Jesus as Lord, allowing him to guide me each step of my life.

That's the distinction Paul made in Galatians 5:16–17:"So I say, *live by the Spirit,* and you will not gratify the desires of the sinful nature. For the sinful nature desires what is contrary to the Spirit, and the Spirit what is contrary to the sinful nature. They are in conflict with each other" (emphasis added).

That's the choice each of us must make if we want a deeply satisfying Christian life. Unfortunately, we don't always choose to walk by the Spirit each step of our journey. I've found two major causes of that. One reason: our humanity encourages us to take the easy road of mediocrity. We'll deal with that after the following section. Another reason: misconceptions, partial truths, and outright untruths about the person, role, and gifts of the Spirit permeate the Christian community.

12 Lies We Hear about the Spirit

I faced most of them. When I discovered the vital role of being filled, my vocabulary didn't include that term. I never would have claimed to be "filled with the Spirit." That was for charismatics and Pentecostals, and I didn't think I fit there since I didn't speak in tongues. Only later, as I grew and continued to learn, did I realize that's what had happened and continues to happen in my life.

But I had to work through a number of untruths about the Spirit. Those untruths must be dealt with if we hope to achieve all that God desires for us. Those untruths have brought confusion and division to the Christian community. But we can focus too much on individual untruths and miss the greater purpose of the Spirit: he wants to lead us into the fullness of God. That's our target.

We'll list the twelve most common misconceptions about the Spirit, with a paragraph that expands on the lie. Then a paragraph or two will summarize the truth about that concept, with a reference to where the book covers that in a little more depth. However, don't expect deep theological expositions about each lie.

After all, I want us to focus on the core of truth about the Spirit, how allowing the Spirit to fill us brings us to the most astoundingly abundant life in Christ. We'll get into that pretty extensively. But let's explore those twelve lies right now.

LIE 1: THE SPIRIT WROTE THE NEW TESTAMENT—AND THEN HE RETIRED

I grew up hearing this one a lot. The premise comes from 1 Corinthians 13:8-10, "Love never fails. But where there are prophecies, they will cease; where there are tongues, they will be stilled; where there is knowledge, it will pass away. For we know in part and we prophesy in part, but when perfection comes, the imperfect disappears." Adherents believe that perfection refers to the New Testament, so at least some of the work of the Spirit was completed at that time. Most adherents believe that the imperfect charismatic gifts passed out of existence then, but some think the Spirit also quit working.

THE TRUTH

Let's just address the last misconception that the Spirit retired. Jesus linked his departure with the continuing presence of the Spirit in lives of his followers in John 14:16-17, "And I will ask the Father, and he will give you another Counselor *to be with you forever*— the Spirit of truth" (emphasis added). The truth? The Spirit didn't retire when he finished one job—he just continues with others.

SEE CHAPTER 1: UNDERSTANDING THE FILLING
THE PROCESS OF BEING FILLED
ALL CHRISTIANS RECEIVE THE SPIRIT

LIE 2: THE SPIRIT WILL TEACH US NEW TRUTH

Like most misconceptions, we can find important biblical truth behind it. Jesus revealed one function of the Spirit in John 16:13, "But when he, the Spirit of truth, comes, he will guide you into all truth." But, just what truth will he guide believers into? New stuff? Or understanding what we study? Some believe in progressive revelation, where the Spirit continues to reveal new truths from God. That means the spiritual landscape can change at any time.

THE TRUTH

Three passages help clarify this misconception. First, the Spirit inspired people to write the New Testament, "Above all, you must understand that no prophecy of Scripture came about by the prophet's own interpretation. For prophecy never had its origin in the will of man, but men spoke from God as they were carried along by the Holy Spirit" (2 Peter 1:20-21). Clearly, the Spirit provides truth for us in scripture.

Second, that scripture possesses all we need to fully develop in the Christian life, "All Scripture is God-breathed and is useful for teaching, rebuking, correcting and training in righteousness, so that the man of God may be *thoroughly equipped for every good work*" (2 Timothy 3:16-17, emphasis added).

Third, the Spirit guides us as we study the truth he's given in the Bible, "Study to shew thyself approved unto God, a workman that needeth not to be ashamed, rightly dividing the word of truth" (2 Timothy 2:15 KJV). The truth? The Bible, provided by the Spirit, has all the truth we need to grow in Christ.

SEE CHAPTER 7: SUPERNATURAL POWER TO DEVELOP INTEGRITY

LIE 3: BEING INDWELT BY THE SPIRIT IS THE SAME AS BEING FILLED

I've been told that we can't get half the Spirit, or 10 percent of him. When we get him, we get the whole enchilada. So when the Spirit comes to live in us, we get him all and can't get any more. As a result, we're filled.

THE TRUTH

Instead, being indwelt and being filled represent two different stages of the spiritual life. According to Acts 2:38, we receive the indwelling presence of the Spirit when we accept Christ, "Repent and be baptized, every one of you, in the name of Jesus Christ for the forgiveness of your sins. And you will receive the gift of the Holy Spirit." (Acts 2:38)

That presence continues. But Paul commands Christians, who have already received the Spirit, to be filled in Ephesians 5:18. "Do not get drunk on wine, which leads to debauchery. Instead, be filled with the Spirit." That makes no sense if we are automatically and continually filled. Furthermore, the verb "be filled" is in the present tense, which means we should regularly allow the Spirit to fill us. The filling isn't a once for all time event. The truth? Receiving the Spirit and being filled represent two distinct experiences.

SEE CHAPTER 1: UNDERSTANDING THE FILLING
THE PROCESS OF BEING FILLED
ALL CHRISTIANS RECEIVE THE SPIRIT
ALL CHRISTIANS CAN BE FILLED WITH THE SPIRIT

LIE 4: BEING FILLED WITH THE SPIRIT IS JUST FOR SOME CHRISTIANS

This lie may have impacted me the most in my struggle. In those days, being filled with the Spirit seemed to be the exclusive domain of charismatics and Pentecostals. So, I never even considered that God wanted me to be filled. Another version of this misconception believes that God fully accepts two levels of Christians: everyday believers who have the Spirit, and disciples who are filled with the Spirit.

THE TRUTH

Actually, God desires that all Christians be filled with the Spirit. In the Ephesians 5 passage above, addressed to believers in general, Paul commanded they be filled. The truth? Being filled with the Spirit is the normal Christian life that God wants for all of his people.

SEE CHAPTER 1: UNDERSTANDING THE FILLING
THE PROCESS OF BEING FILLED
ALL CHRISTIANS RECEIVE THE SPIRIT
ALL CHRISTIANS CAN BE FILLED WITH THE SPIRIT

LIE 5: ALL THE SPIRITUAL GIFTS ARE MENTIONED IN THE NEW TESTAMENT

Once I started exploring the New Testament teachings about the Spirit, I came across Ray Stedman's book *Body Life,* which exposed me to the concept of spiritual gifts. Out of fascination, I began studying them. Most commentators compiled lists and even developed tests to identify which gifts a person possessed. Depending on how they defined them, most lists had about twenty-two gifts. Underlying this, we assumed that the New Testament listed every gift.

THE TRUTH

You may have me here. I can't point to a single passage that contradicts that. But I do present this as my opinion, based on inferences and observations. We can define a spiritual gift as a special ability, imparted by the Spirit after our conversion, to minister and serve the body of Christ. Now, for the inferences. Each list of spiritual gifts is different. Sometimes some gifts overlap, sometimes they don't. That *suggests* that all gifts may not be mentioned, since no New Testament writer thought we needed an exhaustive list. Another inference: Since the Spirit gives gifts as he desires (1 Corinthians 12:11), I feel very uncomfortable in limiting what he gives when the Scriptures don't impose that limit.

I've also observed some followers of Christ with a magnificent ability to minister, that developed after their conversion, that I just can't fit into any of the specific gifts mentioned. Some worship leaders take me right into the presence of God. Others, just as talented and faithful, don't do that. I see that as a spiritual gift, but I can't bend any of the listed gifts to fit there. The Truth? In my opinion, since the Spirit gives as he determines, he can give whatever gift he desires at any time.

SEE CHAPTER 7: SUPERNATURAL POWER TO DEVELOP
     INTEGRITY
    UNIQUELY GIFTED

LIE 6: YOUR SPIRITUAL GIFT WON'T CHANGE

This one comes close to the above lie. Both represent fundamental assumptions about gifts that Scripture doesn't support. And both don't have any one particular verse to contradict them. But many believe that when the Spirit gives a gift, that gift remains operative throughout your life. So, if the Spirit gifts you as a teacher, you continue to teach. If the Spirit gifts you as a pastor, you continue to pastor. Not necessarily in a formal role, but in actions.

THE TRUTH

We assume this, since nothing in Scripture supports it. But can we find inferences and observations again? I think so. Once more, if the Spirit gives as he wills, he can take and add whatever gift(s) he desires at any time. Let's not limit him. At one point in my life, I felt very gifted as a youth pastor. That passed. Later, I felt gifted as a pastor/teacher, but I truly don't sense a gifting as pastor at this point. Either I never had it, but served in that role out of my human strength, or God provided a temporary gifting. I lean toward the latter. The truth? In my opinion, since the Spirit gives as he determines, he can give or take whatever gift he desires at any time.

SEE CHAPTER 7: SUPERNATURAL POWER TO DEVELOP
              INTEGRITY
           UNIQUELY GIFTED

LIE 7: EACH ONE GETS ONE—JUST ONE

Once again we come up against an assumption. Do you get the feeling that a lot of assumptions assail us? That's okay, as long as we don't assume them to be absolute truth for all people at all times. Has anyone asked you, "What's your spiritual gift?" Rarely do I hear "What are your spiritual gifts?" The misconception is that we just have one spiritual gift.

THE TRUTH

Once more, we can find no scripture to indicate this. But we can find many that contradict it. Let's focus on specific gifts identified with Paul. Paul was: an apostle (Galatians 1:1); a prophet (Acts 13:1); a teacher (Acts 13:1); an evangelist (1 Corinthians 1:17); a speaker in tongues (1 Corinthians 14:18); a miracle worker (Acts 19:11); a healer (Acts 19:12); and able to distinguish spirits (Acts 19:12). The truth? Pretty clearly, the Spirit can and has given more than one gift to an individual.

SEE CHAPTER 7: SUPERNATURAL POWER TO DEVELOP
              INTEGRITY
           UNIQUELY GIFTED

LIE 8: THE SPIRIT UNITES CHRISTIANS

This one and the next can be tricky, since they deal with the difference between the ideal and the real. Does the Spirit want to unite Christians? Absolutely true, according to 1 Corinthians 12:13, "For we were all baptized by one Spirit into one body—whether Jews or Greeks, slave or free—and we were all given the one Spirit to drink." So, what makes this a lie? How we practice this unity. Or, rather, how we don't.

THE TRUTH

A spiritual revolution began in the late 1960s, composed primarily of the Jesus Movement and the growing influence of charismatic and Pentecostal churches. People started to think about the Spirit and get excited about him. For many, he just hadn't been a factor in their lives. He now brought a freshness and exuberance to their faith, and people wanted to share that.

And the Spirit, desiring and working for our unity, became a source of division. Churches split over the reality of the charismatic gifts. Are tongues for today? Should all Christians speak in tongues? What about the baptism of the Spirit? Healing? Miracles? Christians broke into multiple camps. And to some extent, that controversy goes on today. The truth? We don't always live in the unity for which the Spirit yearns.

SEE CHAPTER 9: SUPERNATURAL POWER TO TRANSCEND DIFFERENCES

LIE 9: THE SPIRIT DIVIDES CHRISTIANS

Let's flip the story. Even today, many Christians view the Spirit as a disruptive influence. They've seen the damage that disagreement brings, and they move away from any chance of that infecting them. So, they just don't mention the Spirit much at all. Or when they do, they do it safely. A large church in our area had just begun a new series on the book of Acts, and the pastor came to the story of Pentecost, the birthday of the church. This was the first mention of speaking in tongues, and the pastor slid right over it. He merely said, "Pentecostals shouldn't use Acts 2 to justify speaking in tongues, but 1 Corinthians. And that's all we're going to say about it."

THE TRUTH

Even though our practice has made an apparent lie that the Spirit unites us, he truly does. Remember our last verse, "For we were all baptized by one Spirit into one body—whether Jews or Greeks, slave or free—and we were all given the one Spirit to drink." Because all Christians share the Spirit, we are united. Period. We need to live that, and express that. May we obey Paul's command, "Make every effort to keep the unity of the Spirit through the bond of peace" (Ephesians 4:3). The truth? The Spirit and his gifts should unite us.

SEE CHAPTER 9: SUPERNATURAL POWER TO TRANSCEND DIFFERENCES

LIE 10: CHRISTIANS DON'T GENUINELY SPEAK IN TONGUES

This lie flows logically from the more extreme position of Lie 1: The Spirit Wrote the New Testament—and Then He Retired. If the charismatic gifts truly did end with the completion of the New Testament, then any expression of them today cannot be valid. I've even heard some say that speaking in tongues is demonic. Others would say emotion drives it, or that people speak in tongues because others tell them they should. They sometimes "teach" them how to do it.

THE TRUTH

I find it difficult to rule out all speaking in tongues for today. First, Paul told us in 1 Corinthians 14:39, "Therefore, my brothers, be eager to prophesy, and *do not forbid speaking in tongues*" (emphasis added). We can find nothing in this verse that even implies, "don't forbid speaking in tongues until we finish writing the New Testament." Even the passage about the imperfect passing away when the perfect comes can't be conclusively linked to the New Testament, so we shouldn't build significant doctrine on assumptions. The truth? Nothing in the New Testament clearly says that tongues cannot be genuine.

SEE CHAPTER 6: SUPERNATURAL POWER TO DEVELOP INDIVIDUALITY
UNIQUELY GIFTED
EACH BELIEVER HAS ONE (OR MORE!)

LIE 11: YOU CAN'T BE A CHRISTIAN IF YOU DON'T SPEAK IN TONGUES

I heard this frequently in the ferment of the early days of the renewed interest in the Spirit. Some found such joy that they generalized that *all* people could and should gain the same joy in the same way. Some denominations even believe that speaking in tongues is *the* evidence that you possess the Spirit.

THE TRUTH

This just doesn't square with scripture. 1 Corinthians 12:29-30 makes that obvious. "Are all apostles? Are all prophets? Are all teachers? Do all work miracles? Do all have gifts of healing? Do all speak in tongues? Do all interpret?" Just logically, we know that all aren't apostles, and that answer fits all the questions. Even more significantly, the original language of Greek begins each rhetorical question with a word that requires a negative answer. The NASB expresses that well, "All are not apostles, are they? All are not prophets, are they? All are not teachers, are they? All are not *workers of* miracles, are they? All do not have gifts of healings, do they? All do not speak with tongues, do they? All do not interpret, do they?" The truth? Not all Christians should speak in tongues.

SEE CHAPTER 6: SUPERNATURAL POWER TO DEVELOP INDIVIDUALITY
UNIQUELY GIFTED
EACH BELIEVER HAS ONE (OR MORE!)

LIE 12: THE BAPTISM OF THE SPIRIT IS THE SAME AS THE FILLING OF THE SPIRIT

Jesus himself said the 120 disciples would receive the baptism of the Spirit, "Do not leave Jerusalem, but wait for the gift my Father promised, which you have heard me speak about. For John baptized with water, but in a few days you will be baptized with the Holy Spirit" (Acts 1:4-5). That occurred soon after, on the Day of Pentecost, and look at how that event is described in the next chapter,

When the day of Pentecost came, they were all together in one place. Suddenly a sound like the blowing of a violent wind came from heaven and filled the whole house where they were sitting. They saw what seemed to be tongues of fire that separated and came to rest on each of them. All of them were filled with the Holy Spirit and began to speak in other tongues as the Spirit enabled them.
(Acts 2:1–4)

So, Jesus predicted the baptism, and when it happened it was called the filling. Seems logical, doesn't it? Many today equate the two, and use them interchangeably.

THE TRUTH

The two events are quite similar, but when we examine all the New Testament says about each, we find some differences. Only twice does Scripture describe an event as the baptism of the Spirit: the initial outpouring to the 120 original disciples, and the initial outpouring to the Gentiles in Acts 10. Those both seemed to be acts that God initiated. But we frequently read about being filled. Scripture commands believers to be filled, never to receive the baptism of the Spirit. I see the filling as a large circle, with the baptism one specific type of being filled. The truth? Although the filling and the baptism of the Spirit are similar, they have important differences.

SEE CHAPTER 1: UNDERSTANDING THE FILLING
WHAT ABOUT THE BAPTISM OF THE SPIRIT?

When we couple this confusion about the Spirit with our innate desire to be content with mediocrity, then we face a significant double-barreled threat to our spiritual development.

Our Natural Tendency: Boring Christianity

To paraphrase Thoreau, any semi-astute observer can see that "most Christians lead lives of quiet mediocrity."

For some, Christianity is a duty. A good and necessary duty, but not something to get excited about. According to the apostle Paul in 1 Corinthians 3:1–3, many believers allow themselves to be pulled in two directions: "Brothers, I could not address you as spiritual but as worldly—mere infants in Christ. I gave you milk, not solid food, for you were not ready for it. Indeed, you are still not yet ready. You are still worldly. For since there is jealousy and quarreling among you, are you not worldly?"

Paul divides these Christian brothers and sisters into two groups: spiritual Christians and worldly Christians. The worldly ones grabbed onto God with one hand, and to the world with the other. They didn't fully surrender to God.

As a result, they missed out on the best God offers. Because they weren't willing to let go of the world, they could make little progress toward closeness with God.

Like the believers in Paul's time, many Christians today find themselves missing out on supernatural living. Statistics on how many believers live this way really don't matter. The point is: Do you find yourself living a mediocre Christian life? Do *you* yearn for something deeper, more challenging? If so, then avoid the mistake Bart made, which I shared in a previous book.

An intelligent and cautious fourth-grader from the city, Bart spent one summer visiting his country cousins. Finally, they asked if he wanted to ride their horse Champ, and Bart jumped at the chance.

Up close, the horse was much larger than those Bart had seen in cowboy movies. Deciding to get on the horse one small step at a time, he climbed onto a rail fence next to the horse in order to mount him. With one foot firmly planted on the fence, Bart threw his other foot over the saddle.

Champ didn't quite know what to make of this new way to be mounted. He slowly edged away from the fence, pulling part of Bart with him. Bart's caution kept him on the fence; his desire for adventure kept him on the horse—for a short time.

But his nine-year-old legs couldn't stretch forever. Soon he was deposited on the pasture, which was filled with what pastures are usually filled with. Why did he fall? He wasn't willing to fully surrender to the process of getting on the horse.

We confront that same dilemma in the Christian life. If we try to hold on to both the world and God, we fall into "bad stuff." Being filled with the Spirit means getting on the horse without holding onto the fence.

Jesus vividly described half-hearted Christians in Revelation 3:15–16: "I know your deeds, that you are neither cold nor hot. I wish you were either one or the other! So, because you are lukewarm—neither hot nor cold—I am about to spit you out of my mouth."

If we had talked with these church members in Laodicea, I am sure they would have proclaimed both allegiance to and love of Christ. But that wasn't enough. Jesus wants a fire in the soul that burns so brightly the glow can be seen on the outside.

Powered by Gusto

Spiritual gusto comes when we surrender fully to God, when we accept both his goals and his methods for our lives, when we get off the fence to which Bart wanted to stay anchored, and jump onto the horse. Passion comes as we choose to be single-minded in our pursuit of God, when we are willing to go anywhere, be anything, and do anything he desires.

The Bible calls this way of life being led by or filled with the Spirit. Only when the Spirit fills us can his fruit flourish in us. After discussing the fruit of the Spirit in Galatians 5:22–23, Paul concludes with a powerful description of the distinction between the Spirit-led life and the self-led life, in verses 24 and 25: "Those who belong to Christ Jesus have crucified the sinful nature with its passions and desires. Since we live by the Spirit, let us keep in step with the Spirit."

According to Paul, what is the solution to being torn in two directions? To surrender to God, or to allow God's Spirit to lead us in one direction, one step at a time. Remember our earlier warning from verses 16 and 17: either we gratify our sinful nature, or we gratify God's Holy Spirit. We can't do both, and our degree of passion for God comes from that choice.

Where do you stand? Are you ready to fully surrender to God, to say yes to whatever he says? If so, then join us in our search for the truth about supernatural living.

Section I

What is Supernatural Living?

Misconceptions abound regarding what it means to be filled with the Spirit. Some think being filled doesn't apply to them, since they are not charismatic. They don't seek it because they fear they will have to speak in tongues or do something even more dramatic.

Others are convinced that being filled with the Spirit will necessarily result in other manifestations of what we commonly call the charismatic gifts. They find it hard to conceive of being filled and not expressing it in that manner.

Let me suggest a different approach. God wants to fill all of his followers with his Spirit, on a regular basis. This represents the "normal Christian life," and empowers us all to live and to enjoy the Christian life. God wants all believers to be filled, all the time. We may or may not have or manifest the charismatic gifts, but God wants all of us to be filled.

But what does it mean to be filled with God's Spirit? Let's find out.

Chapter 1

Understanding the Filling

Perhaps I only sneaked an occasional sip of Dad's beer in high school, but that wasn't true during my college wanderings. After playing an intramural basketball game, some of us went to a local pizza parlor to "replenish lost liquids." I had a little too much liquid refreshment, and gained a new experience I wouldn't wish on anyone. The exuberance induced by alcohol easily overcame my natural shyness; I became entranced. Back at the dorm we tossed pillows at one another. Although they seemed to slowly float through the air toward me, I still couldn't put my hands together quickly enough to catch one.

As you can imagine, the penalty I paid the next day far exceeded any pleasure I received the night before. Please don't think I recommend that anyone else experience my foolishness. But in his grace, God later used that experience to teach me something about being filled with the Spirit.

On the Day of Pentecost in Acts 2:1–4, a sound like that of a violent wind was heard, tongues like fire touched the heads of the disciples, they were filled with the Holy Spirit, and they spoke in other languages. This event created such a stir that thousands of people rushed to the scene to investigate the situation;

once there, they were amazed at these Christians and their behavior.

How did the unbelievers first interpret this behavior? "Utterly amazed, they asked: 'Are not all these men who are speaking Galileans? Then how is it that each of us hears them in his own native language ... declaring the wonders of God in our own tongues!'" (vv. 7–8, 11). But then look at verse 13: "Some, however, made fun of them and said, 'They have had too much wine.'" Their behavior was suspiciously close to drunkenness. In verses 14 through 21 Peter immediately denied they were drunk, since it was only nine in the morning (much too soon for normal people to be drunk), and identified this unusual behavior as the result of being filled with the Holy Spirit. Incidentally, in Ephesians 5:18 Paul also links and contrasts drinking with being filled: "Do not get drunk on wine, which leads to debauchery. Instead, be filled with the Spirit."

I was struck by the similarity the unbelievers noticed between drunkenness and being filled with the Spirit of God. What caused this confusion?

Speaking in a number of different languages could easily be misconstrued as the slurred speech of drunkenness. Many of us have experienced an inability to quiet a loud drunk, and as we will discover later, being filled with the Spirit generally results in telling people about Jesus. So, part of this confusion could flow from the speech of the apostles.

But we find another attribute of being filled with the Spirit that likewise connects with drunkenness: joyful exuberance. In Galatians 5:22, the second aspect of the fruit of the Spirit mentioned there is joy. Romans 14:17 also connects the Spirit and joy: "For the kingdom of God is not a matter of eating and drinking, but of righteousness, peace and *joy in the Holy Spirit*" (emphasis added). I can't help but think that at least part of the drunkenness charge came from the exuberant joy experienced by the disciples.

Exuberant joy should be a part of the believer's life. I am struck with David's joy when he returned the ark of the covenant to Jerusalem: "David, wearing a linen ephod, danced before the

LORD with all his might" (2 Samuel 6:14). David experienced an exuberance that couldn't be controlled. Again, that sounds a bit like getting drunk.

Without at all recommending that you experience drinking too much, being filled produces a similar exuberance. Why else would the Bible twice link the two experiences? As we choose to walk anywhere the Spirit leads, we can have a greater zest than I experienced; a joy like the apostles experienced, without the disobedience, embarrassment, and hangover that accompany drunkenness.

God desires that we have exuberance in our faith. Once we have had a taste of the joy the Spirit brings to our lives, why would we want to go back to a lukewarm, resistant walk with God? As we are filled with the Spirit, we want more of God. We realize that in order to get more of God, he needs to get more of us. This is how we "grab onto God's gusto," by getting involved in that lifelong process of walking step by step with his Spirit.

The Process of Being Filled

The process of being filled begins at conversion, when a person accepts Jesus Christ as Savior and Lord. At that point every Christian receives a life-changing gift: the Holy Spirit.

ALL CHRISTIANS RECEIVE THE SPIRIT

Listen to the promise given to all Christians, as found in Acts 2:38: "Peter replied, 'Repent and be baptized, every one of you, in the name of Jesus Christ for the forgiveness of your sins. And you *will receive the gift of the Holy Spirit*'" (emphasis added). At the time we give our lives to God, his Holy Spirit comes to live in us. This occurs for each Christian, not just some. But who is this Spirit? Without going into an in-depth description, let's examine some essential truths about the Spirit.

First, he is fully God, according to 2 Corinthians 3:17: "Now the Lord [referring here to Jesus] is the Spirit." Then in Colossians 2:9 we read: "For in Christ all the fullness of the Deity lives in bodily form." So likewise all the traits of God are fully found in his Spirit.

Second, as God, the Holy Spirit is a person, not an impersonal force like a radar beam.

The Spirit possesses the *qualities* of a person. He has his own unique mind: "And he who searches our hearts knows *the mind of the Spirit*" (Romans 8:27, emphasis added). Having a mind, the Spirit operates in the realm of thoughts. Particularly, he even grasps the thoughts of God: "No one *knows the thoughts of God* except the Spirit of God" (1 Corinthians 2:11, emphasis added). The Spirit has his own unique desires, and makes choices flowing from them. The Spirit decides who receives which spiritual gifts: "All these are the work of ... the ... Spirit, and he gives them to each one, *just as he determines*" (1 Corinthians 12:11, emphasis added).

The Spirit also *acts like a person.* He loves people, just as the Father does: "I urge you, brothers, by our Lord Jesus Christ and by *the love of the Spirit*" (Romans 15:30, emphasis added, see also 1 John 4:7-18 about the God of love). He can be communicated with, either honestly or falsely: "Then Peter said, 'Ananias, how is it that Satan has so filled your heart that you have *lied to the Holy Spirit?*'" (Acts 5:3, emphasis added).

When our lives don't match the Spirit's holiness, he experiences disappointment: "And do not *grieve the Holy Spirit of God,* with whom you were sealed for the day of redemption" (Ephesians 4:30, emphasis added). And when we abandon the Christian faith, we insult him: "How much more severely do you think a man deserves to be punished who has ... *insulted the Spirit of grace?*" (Hebrews 10:29, emphasis added).

This is the being who comes to live in us when we come to Christ. Jesus described this indwelling Spirit in John 14:17: "But you know him, for he lives with you and will be in you." God himself, in the form of the third Person of the Trinity, actually lives inside each us as believers. Wherever we go, he goes. Whatever we do, he is there with us and in us.

All Christians receive this tremendous gift of the indwelling Holy Spirit. But not all Christians fully surrender; not all are "on fire for God." Some remain worldly believers, who are still infants (see 1 Corinthians 3:1-3). They have the presence of the Spirit, but not the fruit of the Spirit. Why? Because they haven't completed the process. They have *received* the Spirit, but they have not been *filled with* the Spirit. To do that, they need to fully surrender to the Spirit.

ALL CHRISTIANS CAN BE FILLED WITH THE SPIRIT

In Ephesians 5:18, Paul simply commands Christians to go deeper in the Christian life: "Do not get drunk on wine. ... Instead, be filled with the Spirit." Paul clearly phrased that directive as a general command for all believers. It is not an optional item that can be chosen or rejected; it is part of the normal Christian life. Paul would have no need to command something that intrinsically happens to all Christians, so being filled is not automatic. Nor would he command something of all Christians that is only available to some. Therefore, being filled is intended for and is within the control of each Christian.

In the next chapter we will explore how we can be filled, but what does it mean to be filled with the Spirit? The grammar in the original text of Ephesians 5:18 indicates that being filled is not something that is done once for all, in which one filling completes the job. We go through one wedding ceremony; it lasts for a lifetime without needing to be repeated. But we express our love to our mate every day. Doing so just once and never again won't build a solid relationship. Being filled is the same. Rather than a once for all time event, being filled must be repeated to receive the maximum benefit.

We become filled with the Spirit when we allow him access to and control over all aspects of our lives, when our heart's cry is to please him. Perhaps the best clue to being filled is found in Galatians 5:25: "Since we live by the Spirit, let us *keep in step* with the Spirit" (emphasis added). We fill our lives with the Spirit when we follow him each step of our lives.

The Normal Christian Life

In researching this book, I examined all the biblical passages where being filled with the Spirit is mentioned, and I was surprised to discover how often it occurs. Ephesians 5:18

says that being filled is the normal Christian life, but the rest of the New Testament *demonstrates* that fact. Now, I frequently wonder how any believer can hope to live the Christian life without consciously and intentionally being filled with the Holy Spirit. Let's explore that point.

In the Bible we find prominent believers who were filled. We also find ordinary believers who were filled. We find major events linked with being filled. In examining these various people and events, I hope your perception of the Christian life will be expanded, as was mine.

JOHN THE BAPTIST: FILLED WITH THE SPIRIT

We all recognize the key role John the Baptist played in getting people ready for Jesus. John was a strange individual, clothed with animal skins, eating bugs and wild honey, and living as a hermit (see Matthew 3:1-6). Why did people listen to this unusual character? They saw his spiritual depth and character. Where did that depth and character come from? John was filled with the Spirit even in his mother's womb (see the footnote to Luke 1:15 in the NIV Bible). When Mary visited her cousin, then pregnant with John, Elizabeth was filled with the Spirit (see Luke 1:41). After John's birth, his father Zechariah was likewise filled with the Spirit and prophesied (see Luke 1:67-80). Being filled with the Spirit provided the foundation for the ministry of John.

JESUS: FILLED WITH THE SPIRIT

Jesus first went public when he requested that John baptize him. With crowds of people around, the Holy Spirit descended on Jesus like a dove, and God's voice boomed, "You are my Son, whom I love; with you I am well pleased" (Luke 3:22). That same Holy Spirit then led Jesus into the wilderness to be tempted. How did Jesus begin his ministry? Luke 4:1 says he was full of the Holy Spirit. Jesus' lifesaving ministry began with being filled with the Spirit.

THE CHURCH: FILLED WITH THE SPIRIT

We call the Day of Pentecost the birthday of the church because three thousand people accepted Christ and were baptized that day. That is impressive! How did that day begin? With the disciples being filled with the Spirit (see Acts 2:4), which fulfilled a prophecy made centuries before by a prophet named Joel (see Joel 2:28-32). As evidence, read Acts 2:16-17, in which Peter quoted this prophecy, explaining that the pouring out of God's Spirit on all people (another term for being filled) has always been a part of God's plan—not a revision, but an original.

PETER AND JOHN: FILLED WITH THE SPIRIT

The early church continued to grow explosively, even when faced with significant official opposition. In Acts 3 and 4, Peter and John healed a crippled beggar, the news spread, and the Jewish officials became upset. They thought they had ended this "Jesus nonsense" by having Jesus arrested, convicted, and crucified. The highest Jewish religious officers arrested Peter and John and dragged them into court.

These simple, unlearned fishermen, these "ordinary men" from the rural province of Galilee, were required to defend themselves before the "Supreme Court of Israel" (see Acts 4:1-7). How did they do? Quite well! The court members were astonished at their courage and communication, and were forced to release them (see Acts 4:13-21). What was the secret of the disciples' success in this situation? Peter was filled with the Holy Spirit (see Acts 4:8).

When Peter and John were freed, they continued to tell people about Jesus. Again, they were dragged into court; again, they were released. They went back to the believers and reported what had happened. And the filling spread, but not just among the apostles this time: "After they prayed, the place where they were meeting was shaken. And *they were all filled with the Holy Spirit* and spoke the word of God boldly" (Acts 4:31, emphasis added).

WAITERS: FILLED WITH THE SPIRIT

By chapter 6 of the book of Acts, growth had brought significant problems to the believers. The church divided into contentious groups, focusing on unequal food distribution. If left unchecked, that situation could easily have derailed the early church from carrying out its mission. The apostles created a solution: seven people were selected to serve as waiters, to oversee passing out the food, so the apostles could focus on teaching and prayer (see Acts 6:1–2). What was the first job qualification for these waiters? To be full of the Spirit (see Acts 6:3). What was the result of putting Spirit-filled men into a "menial" job? "The number of disciples … increased rapidly, and a large number of priests became obedient to the faith" (Acts 6:7).

STEPHEN: FILLED WITH THE SPIRIT

The first waiter mentioned was Stephen. And more than being just a waiter, he "did great wonders and miraculous signs among the people" (Acts 6:8). Like Peter and John before him, he was also taken before the high court and ordered to explain himself. This waiter then detailed God's salvation history, culminating in Jesus.

Once again, Stephen was described as "full of the Holy Spirit" as he looked into heaven and saw Jesus at the right hand of God (see Acts 7:55). The court finally lost all patience with these followers of Jesus. Their anger swelled, they dragged Stephen out of the city and stoned him, making him the first Christian martyr. How did this Spirit-filled person react to his rapidly approaching death? He asked God to forgive his slayers (see Acts 7:59–60).

PAUL: FILLED WITH THE SPIRIT

If Peter, filled with the Spirit, led the early Jewish church, God had another in mind to reach the non-Jews. A young Christian-hating and Christian-killing Pharisee named Saul had his Damascus road experience with the resurrected Jesus and became a follower (see Acts 9:1–9). God prepared a mentor for this new Christian who made the task clear to Saul: "Brother Saul, the Lord—Jesus, who appeared to you on the road as you were coming here—has sent me so that you may see again and be filled with the Holy Spirit" (Acts 9:17). What was the foundation of ministry for this man Saul who became known as Paul and "turned the world upside down" (Acts 17:6 KJV)? Being filled with the Spirit.

BARNABAS: FILLED WITH THE SPIRIT

The church continued to grow, as did the persecution. Some disciples fled to the city of Antioch, about four hundred miles north of Jerusalem. There they kept telling people about Jesus, and soon new converts were being made. These new Greek Christians concerned the apostles in Jerusalem, so they sent a reliable young man named Barnabas to Antioch to investigate the situation. His qualifications? "He was a good man, *full of the Holy Spirit* and faith, and a great number of people were brought to the Lord" (Acts 11:24, emphasis added).

MISSIONARIES: FILLED WITH THE SPIRIT

Barnabas recruited another Spirit-filled teacher, Paul, and the Antioch church continued to grow. While five prophets and teachers in the church worshipped and fasted, the Holy Spirit called Barnabas and Paul to be the first intentional missionaries (see Acts 13:1–3). In Paphos they met significant opposition from a magician named Elymas, and Paul took very direct control of the situation. What powered that boldness on the part of Paul? He was filled with the Holy Spirit (see Acts 13:9).

The missionary journey continued, finally reaching another city named Antioch, this one in the heart of current Turkey, then known as Asia Minor. Many in the city believed, causing the Jews there to stir up enough persecution to expel Paul and Barnabas from the town (see Acts 13:13–50). How did they react to this apparent setback? "And the disciples were filled with joy and with the Holy Spirit" (Acts 13:52). How could they respond with joy? Because they were filled with the Spirit and were able to continue their journey to tell more people about Jesus.

REVIEW OF BEING FILLED

Let's overview this history of how being filled builds a foundation for the Christian life. John the Baptist prepared people for the ministry of Jesus by being filled. His mother and father were filled as well. Jesus began his ministry by being filled. The church began at Pentecost by being filled. The Jerusalem church grew and dealt with opposition by being filled, specifically including Peter, John, and Stephen. The Gentile church was begun by people like Barnabas and Paul who were filled with the Spirit. The missionary outreach continued by the filling of the Spirit. Ephesians 5:18 commands each Christian to be filled with the Spirit.

How can we begin to think we can even live the Christian life, let alone be victorious in it and tell others about it, without being filled? Truly, being filled with the Spirit is the normal Christian life. Being filled allows us to "grab God's gusto." Being filled allows us to access God's power to do ministry. Being filled moves us beyond spiritual mediocrity into joyful exuberance.

Being filled with the Spirit sounds like a good thing, doesn't it?

Fearing the Filling

But the concept of being filled may frighten some of us. We may have seen excesses that come with overemphasizing the Spirit; rather than being attracted, we may be confused or even repelled. We have seen that speaking in tongues accompanied the outpouring of the Spirit on the Day of Pentecost, and perhaps we don't want to do that. Can we be filled without it? We know good Christians who don't speak in tongues; is it possible that they are filled? Some say we need to be baptized in the Spirit in order to experience joyful exuberance. But we were baptized in water; isn't that the same, or enough? Is being filled the same as being baptized in the Spirit?

Many of us have been confused by exploring the things of the Spirit. Let's try to eliminate some confusion by seeing what the Bible says that being filled with the Holy Spirit is *not*.

NOT CHARISMATIC GIFTS

Being filled with the Spirit does not mean speaking in tongues. But how do we know that? Clearly, on the Day of

Pentecost the apostles spoke in tongues when they were filled with the Spirit; but should all Christians expect to speak in tongues when they are filled? Think back to Ephesians 5:18, which commands each Christian to be filled with the Spirit. That verse yields our foundational premise: being filled is intended for *all* Christians.

That fact brings up our question: Is speaking in tongues normal for all Christians? If not, then one can be filled without speaking in tongues. We need just one passage to answer that question, 1 Corinthians 12:28–30:

> And in the church God has appointed first of all apostles, second prophets, third teachers, then workers of miracles, also those having gifts of healing, those able to help others, those with gifts of administration, and those speaking in different kinds of tongues. Are all apostles? Are all prophets? Are all teachers? Do all work miracles? Do all have gifts of healing? *Do all speak in tongues?* Do all interpret? (emphasis added).

The logic is inescapable. We agree that not all Christians are apostles. We agree that not all Christians are prophets. Following the same logic, not all Christians speak in tongues. The grammar is likewise inescapable. The original language makes each of these statements a rhetorical question that requires a negative answer. Go back to our question: Is speaking in tongues normal for all Christians? The clear biblical answer is no.

So, if you are a non-charismatic reader, you can breathe a deep sigh of relief. You can be filled without speaking in tongues. These are two different experiences: Being filled is for all; speaking in tongues is not.

If you are a charismatic reader, you can likewise relax. This passage is not an attack on the scriptural use of charismatic gifts today. We have seen enough division from both sides. Do some validly speak in tongues today? I believe so. Good friends and trusted brothers in Christ have been blessed by the practice. Our goal here is to discover not how every Christian can speak in tongues, but how every Christian can be filled with the Holy Spirit—on a regular, recurring basis.

Having cleared up that question to the satisfaction of all (hopefully!), let's consider another issue that has long brought confusion regarding being filled with the Spirit.

WHAT ABOUT THE BAPTISM OF THE SPIRIT?

Just what is the baptism of the Holy Spirit? Some believe it is synonymous with being filled with the Holy Spirit. Some believe that the baptism of the Holy Spirit occurred only in the first century. Let's briefly try to clear up this confusion. First, the concept of the baptism of the Holy Spirit is important. Even though each Gospel writer chooses to present various events and not to mention others, each of these biblical writers quoted John the Baptist's prediction that Jesus would baptize with the Holy Spirit (see Matthew 3:11; Mark 1:8; Luke 3:16; John 1:33).

Jesus also predicted that he would do so. After his resurrection and before his ascension into heaven he told his disciples, "In a few days you will be baptized with the Holy Spirit" (Acts 1:5), looking forward to the Day of Pentecost. Jesus also described this event as "when the Holy Spirit comes on you" (Acts 1:8). That phrase "come on" (or "came on") is used later in Acts 10:44 and 11:15. So we find all four Gospel writers and Jesus specifically mentioning the baptism of the Holy Spirit. That point is significant; we can't ignore it.

LINKED TO THE FILLING

Also, a clear link exists between the filling and the baptism. Jesus said the disciples would be baptized with the Spirit, which later occurred on the Day of Pentecost. Of the numerous events of that day, Acts 2:4 also describes the disciples being filled with the Spirit. Since both occurred at Pentecost, the biblical accounts are obviously not referring to two totally separate experiences. If not identical, they are at least connected in some way.

DIFFERENT FROM THE FILLING

However, the two experiences have significant differences. Let's begin by examining what happens with each of these events. At Pentecost, a sound like a violent wind was heard, tongues like those of fire rested on those receiving the filling, and they all spoke in tongues, or known languages. Only the last of these three occurrences was ever mentioned as happening again.

The only other specific mention of believers being baptized in the Spirit is found in Acts 10, at the first outreach to non-Jews. Peter shared the Gospel with Cornelius, his friends and family. During the message, the Holy Spirit came upon the non-Jews, and they spoke in tongues and praised God. Peter realized they had received the Spirit just as the original Jewish disciples had done at Pentecost.

In the next chapter Peter explained to the Jewish believers in Jerusalem what had occurred with Cornelius and company:

> As I began to speak, the Holy Spirit came on them as he had come on us at the beginning. Then I remembered what the Lord had said: "John baptized with water, but you will be baptized with the Holy Spirit" (Acts 11:15-16).

This account is only the second specific mention of believers being baptized with the Spirit. Now, if being filled and being baptized with the Spirit are exactly the same thing, we would expect that each of them would have similar results. We have no record of the sound like a violent wind and tongues like fire ever occurring again. Although absence of evidence is not evidence of absence, as awesome as these events are, I tend to think they would have been mentioned if they had ever been repeated.

Tongues occurred at each case of the baptism to confirm the coming of the Holy Spirit. Yet tongues are not normative for all Christians who are filled with the Holy Spirit. That is a significant contrast. So, we find important differences between what happens with the baptism of the Holy Spirit and the filling with the Holy Spirit.

Also, God never tells us to seek being baptized with the Spirit. Instead, those participants in the baptism of the Holy Spirit were passive; something was done to them. And even that something only happened on two occasions in the Bible. But we are told to seek to be filled, and to do that on a regular basis. In that case, we are not passive, but active seekers.

PUTTING THEM TOGETHER

So, how can we synthesize being baptized with the Spirit and being filled with the Spirit? Let me suggest that being baptized is a unique subset within being filled. Here is an example. No motorcycles can match some traits of Harley-Davidsons. Their throaty roar, rumble, and mystique make them *the* motorcycle for many riders. The Harley is a truly unique bike.

All Harleys are motorcycles. But not all motorcycles are Harleys. Honda makes a fine bike (I ride one), as do Yamaha, Suzuki, and others. So how do we connect motorcycles and the Holy Spirit?

Being filled with the Spirit means being fully open to God. Or, being a motorcycle. Two times, at Pentecost when the Spirit first filled the Jerusalem believers, and at Caesarea when the Spirit first filled non-Jewish believers, that form of the filling was described as being baptized with the Spirit. In other words, of being a Harley—unique.

So, although being baptized with the Spirit is part of being filled, one can be filled with the Spirit without being baptized with him. The baptizing was the initial outpouring of the Holy Spirit, on Jewish believers at Pentecost, and on Gentile believers with Cornelius.

Initial acts have no need to be repeated. But being filled is something that is needed again and again. Let's wrap up what it means to be filled with the Spirit.

Continuing, Voluntary Surrender

When we yield ourselves day by day to the Holy Spirit, we recommit ourselves daily to put God first in our lives and to be the person he wants us to be. We also allow the Spirit access to any hidden rooms in our hearts.

In my first book I told the story of a time when my wife Sheila and I had some friends over for dinner. The house was neat, clean, dusted, and freshly vacuumed, and the study doors were firmly closed. Not one of our guests could have guessed that walking into the study meant taking their lives into their hands. We had shoved the loose ends of several unfinished projects in there, hoping no one would look.

Sometimes our spiritual lives are like that example. Inviting Jesus into our lives is somewhat like inviting him into our house. We have cleaned up all the main rooms. At first glance, everything looks pretty good.

But we have a secret junk room where we hide thoughts and acts we don't want him to see. We may even try to deny their existence to ourselves. Usually, those doors have a master lock that would withstand a .357 magnum bullet.

Being filled with the Spirit means that we unlock those locks and open those doors, even when part of us isn't quite ready to do so, because we want God's presence more than anything else. That's being filled. Now, let's discover how we develop gusto in our faith.

Chapter 2

Receiving the Filling

During his walk that led by his neighborhood church, Terry Bradley noticed some shrubs on fire. He ran to the office and told the secretary to call the fire department. She made the call and explained the situation, and the 911 operator responded, "You mean to tell me that there's a burning bush on your church lawn, and you want to put it out?"

What a marvelous picture of how to be filled with the Holy Spirit! We recognize the allusion to God speaking to Moses through a burning bush in Exodus 3. Why would we, the church, want to put out the fire? The reason is twofold: (1) Like Moses, we may not want to hear what God has to say to us. (2) We may not want to do what God wants us to do.

But a willingness to let the fire burn, to hear what God has to say, and to obey, yields the essence of being filled. Using that analogy of fire, let's explore six principles of how to be filled with the Spirit.

Let it Burn

In June 1988, a small lightning-caused fire broke out in Yellowstone National Park. Since the largest previous burn maxed out at 20,000 acres, officials allowed the fire to burn. That decision matched the new policy of allowing natural fires to continue. But by July 14, lightning had ignited other blazes, and they merged into a firestorm; officials then marshaled all their resources to put out the roaring inferno.

The back of the fire wasn't broken until September, when rain and snow began. Only the heavier snows of November put it out fully. By then, about one-third of the park had burned, totaling 800,000 acres. Another 400,000 acres had been destroyed outside the park. Vast damage to wildlife, fish, birds, and trees had occurred.

Why did *this* fire do so much more damage than others before it? Several factors combined, but previous park policy contributed the most. Since the establishment of Yellowstone National Park in 1872, officials had fought fires with all the means available. But by the 1970s, they had learned more about the interaction of fires and forests.

When allowed to burn naturally, fires clear out undergrowth, resulting in less damaging future fires due to less fuel. Lodgepole pines, constituting about 80 percent of the park's forests, require the high heat of fires to release their seeds from the cones. Douglas firs have a thick bark that can protect them against natural fires.

Fires play a vital role in forest development. God designed forests both to withstand and benefit by fires, and stopping fires actually decreases forests' health. So at Yellowstone policy shifted to allow natural fires to burn unchecked for the long-term health of the forest. Unfortunately, years of accumulating undergrowth had provided a rich source of fuel for the 1988 firestorm. Decades of putting out smaller fires resulted in a greater fire later.

Let me suggest we become filled with the Spirit when we let the fire of the Spirit burn in our lives, without trying to put it out. We need to surrender to what God desires for us. First Thessalonians 5:19 follows through on our analogy: "Do not put out the Spirit's fire." Or, don't stop the fire before its time. Not only should we allow the Spirit to burn in our lives, we should allow the Spirit to *keep* burning. Let's look at the context of that verse:

Make sure that *nobody* pays back wrong for wrong, but *always* try to be kind to *each* other and to *everyone* else.

Be joyful *always;* pray *continually;* give thanks in *all* circumstances, for this is God's will for you in Christ Jesus.

Do not put out the Spirit's fire; do not treat prophecies with contempt. Test *everything*. Hold on to the good. Avoid *every* kind of evil (1 Thessalonians 5:15-22, emphasis added).

I counted nine all-inclusive terms in those brief eight verses; each of these highlighted terms flows from allowing the Spirit to do whatever he desires to do in us: *Always. Every. Continually.* When we do as God tells us in this passage, we give our all to receive his all.

This openness provides the key to the abundant Spirit-filled life—if we don't put limits on following what God desires. Remember how Moses fought against God? He made every excuse he could think of to resist him. But finally he "let the fire burn," and God used him mightily.

Jeremiah 29:13 confirms that spiritual principle: "You will seek me and find me when you seek me with all your heart." Seeking God with all our heart means valuing him above all, and being willing to do whatever he says we must do. The Spirit fills us when we allow him to change any part of our lives. Right now, are you doing anything to quench the fire of the Spirit in you? Are you resisting him or holding back from him? If so, then let go, let the fire burn, and step into God's gusto.

Step into the Flames

One of the aspects of the Spirit that I truly appreciate is the fact that he will not come into us to do his purifying work in us without our permission. Jesus himself indicated as much in Luke 11:9-13:

"So I say to you: Ask and it will be given to you; seek and you will find; knock and the door will be opened to you. *For everyone who asks receives;* he who seeks finds; and to him who knocks, the door will be opened.

"Which of you fathers, if your son asks for a fish, will give him a snake instead? Or if he asks for an egg, will give him a scorpion? If you then, though you are evil, know how to give good gifts to your children, how much more will your Father in heaven *give the Holy Spirit to those who ask him!"* (emphasis added).

Does Jesus mean we have to ask God to receive the Holy Spirit when we come to Christ? I don't think so, since God gives the Spirit to all believers automatically at that time (see Acts 2:38). But to receive the filling of the Spirit, we need to request it. In essence, we need to voluntarily stick our finger into the flames. Remember, the grammar of Ephesians 5:18 indicates that the filling doesn't happen just once, but repeatedly.

Jesus made that fact clear in Luke 9:23 when he said another "go all the way" event that needs to be regularly repeated: "If anyone would come after me, he must deny himself and take up his cross *daily* and follow me" (emphasis added). Taking up our cross certainly signifies "going all the way"; we have seen that being filled means allowing the Spirit to stay aflame in our lives. Both events—denying ourselves and taking up our cross, and being filled with the Spirit—need repetition. One time doesn't do it for all time.

Why? Most of us make significant decisions, only to slowly fall back into the rut of our regular behavior. But when we recommit ourselves to God on a daily basis, then we reaffirm our new direction. Each day, we need to recommit to following Jesus. Each day, we need to ask for the Spirit to fill us. Each day, we need to begin to build a new pattern.

Now, let's see what else happens when we ask the Spirit to fill us.

Be Purified by Fire

Compare the underbrush that had built up in Yellowstone to the sins in our lives that have accumulated for years without being dealt with. In Yellowstone, when the conditions combined to bring a spark, devastation followed. Why? The underbrush hadn't been cleared out, and it exploded into flame. The same kind of thing happens to us in regard to our sins.

To be filled with the *Holy* Spirit, we need to yearn for *holiness*. Why? Holiness expresses the character of God, and as followers of Jesus we should desire to imitate him in every way. Choosing a relationship with a holy God involves wanting to develop the same character traits that he has. So we take a major step toward being filled with the Holy Spirit when we yearn for holiness.

That thought runs throughout both the Old and New Testaments: "But just as he who called you is holy, so *be holy* in all you do; for it is written: '*Be holy, because I am holy*'" (1 Peter 1:15, emphasis added). Peter knew his Old Testament. At least four times in Leviticus, God commanded his people to be holy because he is holy (Leviticus 11:44; 19:2; 20:7; 20:26). Like Father, like children.

But holiness means more than just loving holiness; we also need to hate sin. Let's recognize the danger of having the uncleared underbrush of sin in our lives.

Over the years, Charlie built a solid habit of arrogance. His intelligence, skill, and drive easily exceeded that of most, and an attitude of superiority colored how he viewed others. Not even his skill could completely hide his scorn.

Then he joined a group of men in a Bible study on character, and he discovered humility; biblical humility that does not deny the worth of anyone, but values everyone equally. He recognized his failings in this area, and this godly trait immediately attracted him. Yet he made fitful progress in attaining it until one of the men in the group made a suggestion.

"Charlie, do you recognize the damage your arrogance has brought to you and others? How's your relationship with your family with the people at work? Make a list of how your arrogance has brought pain, and read it each day."

That suggestion turned the corner for Charlie; it helped him recognize both the goodness of the good trait, and the evilness of the bad one. Not only did he come to love humility, he also grew to hate sin.

Do we sometimes minimize the damage of sin? Let's accept God's perspective, that it's wrong—always wrong. It always brings damage.

But how do we develop that holiness in practice? How do we move beyond abstract theory? We can be filled with the Spirit only when we allow him to do his work. Jesus talked about the future work of the Spirit in believers: "But I tell you the truth: It is for your good that I am going away. Unless I go away, the Counselor [the Spirit] will not come to you; but if I go, I will send him to you. When he comes, he will *convict the world of guilt in regard to sin* and righteousness and judgment" (John 16:7-8, emphasis added).

I believe that convicting work of the Spirit applies to all those who live in the world. That includes believers. And notice that Jesus said this works for our good.

Part of the Spirit's job deals with pointing out our underbrush, and that process is extremely painful. Facing up to our moral failures brings guilt, shame, and embarrassment. Sometimes we would just as soon pretend they never occurred. But we need the underbrush cleared, and only fire can do that. The Spirit shows the underbrush to us, and we agree it needs to go. He then strikes the match, and asks us to apply it. Once we apply it, he begins to work.

The Bible calls that act of applying the fire to the underbrush confession, repentance, and forgiveness. These are simple terms. In confession we agree with God that our sin is undergrowth and needs to go. In repentance we turn away from our sin so that we don't keep adding to the brush pile. In forgiveness we allow the Holy Spirit to burn it up for a fresh start.

God designed forests to need and withstand regular fires. He also designed us to need and withstand the purifying work of the Spirit in bringing us to holiness. Do you have any underbrush that needs clearing? Have you allowed any sin to accumulate? Learn the lesson of Yellowstone, and regularly allow the Spirit to clean out your life.

Feed the Fire

Back in Boy Scouts, I learned how to build and put out fires. Fire requires three things to burn: heat, oxygen, and fuel. Eliminate any one, and either the fire will not start, or it will go out. If we desire the Spirit to burn in our lives, we must provide the fuel. In the last section, we defined our sins as underbrush that feeds the fire. If we regularly clean out that underbrush, we eliminate the fuel. But since we still want the fire of the Holy Spirit to burn within us, we must add another type of fuel.

Let me suggest that fuel comes both from burning out what shouldn't be there and from adding what should be there. Let's go back to our primary passage on being filled with the Spirit and see what God indicates will provide the fuel for the Spirit to burn.

> And be not drunk with wine, wherein is excess; but *be filled* with the Spirit;
>
> *Speaking* to yourselves in psalms and hymns and spiritual songs, *singing* and *making melody* in your heart to the Lord;
>
> *Giving thanks* always for all things unto God and the Father in the name of our Lord Jesus Christ;
>
> *Submitting* yourselves one to another in the fear of God (Ephesians 5:18-21 KJV, emphasis added).

I quoted the *King James Version* this time because it best expresses the original grammar. The phrase "be filled" is a command. Then Paul explains *how* to be filled. That command is followed by five participles. In English, they typically end in "ing," as we see in the *King James Version*. These terms do not represent separate commands, but five steps we must take in order to carry out the one command to be filled. That is an important distinction. So, according to the text, according to God, how can we obey the command to allow the Spirit to fill us?

I am impressed that he doesn't give us something superspiritual, weird, or impossible to do. Instead, there are five tasks; simple to understand, even if not simple to do: speaking spiritually, singing, making melody in our hearts, giving thanks, and submitting.

The Spirit fills us when we fill our lives with "God stuff": God talk, God praise, God relationships. When we do these things, we give God more of the space in our lives. The Spirit lives there, more and more. That's why all of us can be filled with the Spirit, even if we don't all speak in tongues. We can all do each of these things.

Now let's look at the Spirit's fuel.

SPEAKING SPIRITUALLY

We make room for the Spirit when our conversation focuses on spiritual things, like talking about God's Word and what God is doing in our lives, and avoiding language that damages others. Go back just one chapter in Ephesians, to chapter 4, verses 29–30. Notice again the link between our openness to the Spirit and our speech: "Do not let any unwholesome talk come out of your mouths, but only what is helpful for building others up according to their needs, that it may benefit those who listen. And do not grieve the Holy Spirit of God, with whom you were sealed for the day of redemption."

Unwholesome talk not only grieves the Spirit, it also limits his work in us. If you are an avid football fan or a "clothesaholic," you can relax. God doesn't forbid casual conversation about sports, fashions, and other topics. He just requires that our speech not damage others, and that, along with all the other good things we talk about, we frequently include him!

I have noticed that one of the best ways to craft a romantic evening with my wife is to talk about our early days.

As I ponder what attracted her to me, she becomes more attractive. As I remember difficult times we have worked through, the strength of our relationship becomes more apparent. What's the dynamic here? The more I talk about us, the more space "us" has in my mind.

The connection with our walk with God is just as apparent. When I tell someone about how God showed his love for me, I also become more aware of his love. When I talk with a friend in the Sierra Mountains about the majesty of God as shown in his creation, his majesty becomes a greater part of my consciousness. Or, I become more filled with the Spirit. How? I talk about "God stuff."

SINGING AND MAKING MELODY

Let's combine these two participles; they go together. I particularly like the literal original phrase, "singing and psalming the heart of you." One morning I woke up with a popular praise song running through my mind. In deference to my wife's desire to continue in her sleep, I didn't burst into audible noise. Yes, the word *noise* was intentional.

God never gave me the ability to sing so that others appreciate it. But I appreciate my singing, and I believe he does too. A good friend turned me on to Caedmon's Call, a Christian group with lyrics that express their grapples with key issues of faith. Listening to their poetry set to music has a great impact on me.

I have noticed a dramatic difference in my day when I fill it with songs about God. My attitude improves, I think more about the Lord, and I am more in touch with him. Or, I am more filled with the Spirit. I make four one-hour trips each week to the university where I teach. Part of the time I listen to the traffic reports to discover the status of the Southern California parking lots (we call them "freeways" here) or to sports (remember, that's okay unless it's all we listen to and talk about), but I most enjoy putting on worship CDs and worshipping the Lord along with them.

Music possesses a special ability to reach our hearts and minds simultaneously. Although talking primarily influences our thoughts, music touches our souls. Several years ago I took a motorcycle trip with several friends, and made a small "cheat sheet" of the names of many songs. I didn't have a radio or CB on my bike, as so many other bikers did back then, so I just spent the time "singing and psalming" in my heart. And since no one could hear me, I also did so at full volume. I have rarely experienced a greater intimacy with God.

So, if you love the Spirit and want to be filled, do some singing to God. And if you are in public and love people, please do it silently.

GIVING THANKS

This one gets more difficult and involves some important theology. Don't worry. Theology is just the study of God; we won't get into angels and the heads of pins! Paul links being filled with the Spirit to a continual attitude of thankfulness. Look again at Ephesians 5:20 where he speaks of "always giving thanks to God the Father for everything."

Here Paul gets pretty absolute. The more we thank God for all things, the more filled with his Spirit we become. Why? First, we get God more involved in our lives. We allow him into each event. That action alone increases our being filled. Second, by giving thanks for everything we acknowledge God's sovereignty—not that God causes all things, but he does allow them when they fit within his will; he uses them all.

James 1:2-4 presents a classic expression of this point: "Consider it *pure joy, my brothers, whenever you face trials of many kinds,* because you know that the testing of your faith develops perseverance. Perseverance must finish its work so that you may be mature and complete, not lacking anything" (emphasis added).

We get excited at the good things that God brings to us. That's normal. We also get excited when God changes our lives for the better. How do we get better? By working with God through difficulties. So, if God uses each hard experience to refine us, shouldn't we thank him for what he's doing? And won't that thanks expand our view of him?

Always thanking God exalts our view of him and maximizes our perspective of his loving involvement in every detail of our lives. As we give thanks to God, he fills up more and more of the space in our lives; we get more filled with his Spirit all the time.

SUBMITTING

Each step seems to get more difficult, doesn't it? It's funny how we get filled with God's Spirit when we yield to others. That's what submitting is: overcoming our ingrained self-will and trying to meet other's needs as well as ours. How does this action help us get filled with the Holy Spirit?

Paul provides the answer to that question in Philippians 2:3-8:

> Do nothing out of selfish ambition or vain conceit, but in humility consider others better than yourselves. Each of you should look not only to your own interests, but also to the interests of others.
>
> Your attitude should be the same as that of Christ Jesus: Who, being in very nature God, did not consider equality with God something to be grasped, but made himself nothing, taking the very nature of a servant, being made in human likeness. And being found in appearance as a man, he humbled himself and became obedient to death—even death on a cross!

Jesus gave us the prime example of submitting to the needs of others as an expression of love for God. Can we doubt, then, that when we submit in a similar manner that we grow closer to God, that we become more filled with his Spirit? As we do so, we develop a Spirit-led concern for others. We speak spiritually, when we sing and make melody in our hearts, when we give thanks, when we submit, we feed the fire of the Spirit. We fill our lives with "God stuff," and the Spirit fills us with himself.

Follow the Flames

Some time ago I journeyed to the Sierras for a solo three-day trip. October nights promised a chill, so I sacrificed precious fishing time to gather wood for the evening fire. But I gave the rest of the afternoon to fishing, at least until darkness kept me from seeing my line. I have discovered that I lose a lot of gear fishing a stream with no light, so I headed back to camp.

I prepared an easy meal, then lit the fire and relaxed before it in a camp chair with a cup of hot chocolate. Soon the flames hypnotized me. My eyes followed each spurt of incandescent gas, trying to find a pattern in the swirls of yellow, red, orange, and sometimes blue. I spent hours meditating, thinking, and praying, all the while intently following the path of the flames.

Use that as an analogy of being filled. Love the flames, stay close, and follow where they go. I like the way J. B. Phillips translated 1 Thessalonians 5:19: "Never damp the fire of the Spirit." Clearly, God wants to spark a flame in us, a firestorm that will rage through our lives, consuming the underbrush.

To put it simply, we become filled with the Spirit when we go where the Spirit leads us. We don't resist because we really don't want to follow. We don't look at the bottom line, to see how much it will cost. We don't look for reasons to say no, as Moses did when confronted with the burning bush. But when the Spirit speaks, we listen. We look for reasons to say yes.

That's what the Spirit told us through Paul back in Galatians 5:16, 25: "So I say, live by the Spirit, and you will not gratify the desires of the sinful nature. ... Since we live by the Spirit, let us keep in step with the Spirit."

In our new life in the Spirit, we need to go where he leads, to follow the flames, to say yes rather than no. After I discovered being filled with the Spirit, I soon got into a youth ministry, got burned by church politics, almost as quickly got out, and vowed to serve God doing other things. While I was living in Taos, New Mexico, God used several men in my church to gently nudge me back into ministry. With heels dug in, I fought against it.

I told God, "I've been there, done that; once is enough." He seemed to reply, "What you did isn't what I want you to do."

"But Taos is almost heaven for me. It has mountains, skiing, fishing, solitude."

This time Jesus spoke: "Tim, I did give up heaven. Besides, whatever you give up, I'll restore a hundred times." I seemed to recall a verse that sounded suspiciously like that statement (see Matthew 19:29).

"But, I'm just not qualified."

"Remember Moses? I'll never lead you where I won't guide you, and I won't send you where I won't defend you."

Finally, I gave in. But I should have looked for reasons to say yes to God at first, instead of trying to squirm out. Following the Spirit means following, not fighting. Do you sense the Spirit leading you? Perhaps in a new life direction? Perhaps to change an ingrained habit? Perhaps to forgive a friend who wounded you? If so, how can you best follow the Spirit's leading?

Strike the Match

On that Sierra trip, all my wood gathering and setting of the fire would have done no good if I had not struck the match and applied it to the kindling. In our lives, the Spirit fills us when we take these steps. Have we surrendered to the Spirit? Will we allow him to fill and lead us? Are we ready to burn out some underbrush?

I challenge you now to ask God to fill you with his Spirit on a daily basis. You know how. Now it's time to strike the match.

Section II

Living with Supernatural Power

*"But you will receive power
when the Holy Spirit comes on you."*
—Acts 1:8

A s I pondered this section, I kept coming back to the purpose of our time together. Let's go back to the first paragraphs of the book.

Why do some Christians seem to have no gusto in their faith? They attend church services, they serve the Lord and others, they give of their time and their material possessions, but they never seem to burn with passion for God. They don't dig deep into him. Their faith is genuine, and they love God, but something clearly is missing from their lives.

Other Christians are different. They are no more talented or intelligent, but their lives have a spiritual zest. Passion motivates their actions. They would never claim to be sinless, yet sin seems to become less frequent among them.

The Spirit fills us when we fully allow him to do his work in us. Let's discover the power of the Spirit that transforms our lives.

Chapter 3

Receiving Supernatural Power

I enjoy driving fast. I guess I inherited that trait from my dad; years ago he set a world speed record for driving from New York City to Santa Monica, California. I learned to drive with his 1963 Ford Galaxie 500, a land rocket with a high-compression, 352-cubic-inch, V8 engine. I once raced and beat a Corvette in that car. More recently, I loved pushing our Chrysler LeBaron GTS turbo to its limits. In an emergency, I once drove the thirty miles of curves from our house to a nearby mountain town in less than twenty minutes. Yes, I have received a speeding ticket or two, and no, I don't recommend speeding to anyone. It's illegal, unsafe, and irresponsible. I want to make that point perfectly clear. That's why I no longer do it.

Filled with the Spirit, Filled with Power

Back in the 1970s, I test drove a Lotus Elan, a race-bred sports car. A light touch on the gas, and the car leaped ahead. When cornering, like in the old TV tire commercials, the tires became tiger's claws that reached out, grabbed the asphalt, and pulled. I have never driven anything that responsive in my life.

That Lotus depicts the Christian life far better than a Ford Escort. Although we often feel powerless, we drive the Lotus. We have the power. But we drive it like an Escort: slow, cautious, careful. Perhaps we don't *know* the power that's available, or perhaps we *fear* the difficult spots it may put us in. But knowing that we possess spiritual power tends to remove our excuses.

Let's review. First, all Christians receive the Spirit. That point is pretty basic. Second, all Christians can and should be filled with the Spirit. Now, where does that lead us?

The premise of this chapter is simple: power and the Spirit are inseparable. Power defines the Spirit. When the Spirit arrives, power arrives. Next comes our conclusion: when the Spirit fills us, he fills us with power—power to transform our lives, power to accomplish far more than we have ever dreamed, power to be what God desires of us.

For this chapter, we will study each verse in the NIV Bible that links the Spirit and power. This exercise may surprise you as much as it surprised me.

The Spirit is Power

When I first organized this book, I didn't think of this chapter. But as I moved from the preceding chapter on how to be filled into the next chapter on the practical dimensions of being filled, the writing process came to a halt. The solution to the blockage only came when I realized we need a transition that shows that the Spirit provides the power to change our lives.

I anticipated getting enough material to write a paragraph or two when I entered "Spirit" and "power" in my computer Bible search program. Twenty-two entries directly linked the two. Ten came from the Old Testament, twelve from the New, showing that this principle runs throughout the history of God's involvement with his people.

The Spirit is defined as power in Isaiah 11:2: "The Spirit of the LORD will rest on him—the Spirit of wisdom and of understanding, *the Spirit* of counsel and *of power,* the Spirit of knowledge and of the fear of the LORD" (emphasis added).

We read repeatedly that the Spirit of the Lord came in power upon an individual or a group of people: Samson (see

Judges 14:6; 14:19; 15:14), Saul (see 1 Samuel 10:6; 10:10; 11:6), David (see 1 Samuel 16:13), Mary the mother of Jesus (see Luke 1:35), and the disciples at Pentecost (see Acts 1:8).

I almost missed something I knew well: we just can't separate the two. The Spirit *is* power, and he brings power to the lives of those he indwells. Let's explore some examples of people who chose to drive the Lotus rather than the Escort.

JESUS

Jesus' life divides itself into three major parts: his unique birth, his sinless life, and his unprecedented resurrection. The power of the Spirit enabled all three of these miraculous events. Think just a little about the concept of the Trinity: one God with three discrete Persons—each God, each fully God, but each with a different role. Only a divine Person could do the tasks attributed to the Spirit. And each of these tasks expresses a marvelously close cooperation with the other Persons of the Trinity. Together, they accomplish the salvation of humanity.

Luke 1:35 links the power of the Spirit and the birth of Jesus: "The angel answered [Mary], *The Holy Spirit will come upon you, and the power of the Most High will overshadow you.* So the holy one to be born [Jesus] will be called the Son of God" (emphasis added). The Holy Spirit enabled Jesus' entry into this life.

The ministry of Jesus depended upon the power of the Spirit, according to Luke 4:14: "Jesus returned to Galilee *in the power of the Spirit,* and news about him spread through the whole countryside" (emphasis added, see also Acts 10:38). Although Jesus was the Son of God the Father, he relied upon the power of the Spirit for what he did with people.

The power of the Spirit expressed itself in the resurrection: "And who through the *Spirit of holiness was declared with power to be the Son of God by his resurrection* from the dead: Jesus Christ our Lord" (Romans 1:4, emphasis added).

Paul placed the entire credibility of Christianity upon the reality of Jesus' resurrection in 1 Corinthians 15:17: "And if Christ has not been raised, your faith is futile; you are still in your sins." The Spirit provided the power for the world-changing resurrection.

If the power of the Spirit operated in order for Jesus to be born, to minister, and to be resurrected, doesn't it make sense that we also should benefit from such power? Unless we are content to drive the Escort instead of the Lotus.

LEADERSHIP AND MINISTRY

If Jesus relied upon the power of the Spirit for effective ministry, humans in any form of leadership or ministry need to take advantage of that same source. We have already seen that a prominent Old Testament prophet and the first two kings of Israel experienced the power of the Spirit as they led the nation. Another Old Testament prophet specifically received power from the Spirit: "But as for me, *I am filled with power, with the Spirit of the LORD,* and with justice and might, to declare to Jacob his transgression, to Israel his sin" (Micah 3:8, emphasis added).

Telling people that they are sinning never tops the list of fun things to do. Most of us prefer to avoid confrontation and strife, even when we know they are necessary. How did the prophet Micah overcome that innate desire to avoid offending people? He allowed the Spirit to fill him with power.

Solomon's temple astounded the world because of its glory and grandeur. But that temple had been built with Israel at the height of its glory, and the Babylonian Captivity saw the destruction of the nation and the temple, and the impoverishment of the people. So when Zerubbabel led a campaign to rebuild the temple, discouragement afflicted many of his followers. Zerubbabel possessed neither the finances and royal heritage, nor the power and might of David and Solomon.

God suggested another source of success—the power of the Spirit: "So he said to me, 'This is the word of the LORD to Zerubbabel:'Not by might nor by power, but by my Spirit,' says the LORD Almighty'" (Zechariah 4:6).

Although human power couldn't provide the resources to rebuild the temple, the Spirit provided the power, and the temple was built.

Moving into the New Testament, we see a marvelous ministry by Paul. First opposed to the followers of Jesus, he became the foremost proponent, the first missionary, and a church planter. His ministry was so successful that an opponent later referred to him and his companions as "these that have turned the world upside down" (Acts 17:6 KJV).

What powered Paul's effectiveness? He tells us in his own words: "My message and my preaching were not with wise and persuasive words, but with a demonstration of the Spirit's power" (1 Corinthians 2:4, see also Romans 15:18-19; 1 Thessalonians 1:4-5).

Paul had an excellent education, a keen mind, and a classically driven Type A personality. He yearned to get things done. But what did *he* think allowed him to be effective? The power of the Spirit. We see key leaders with their ministry empowered by the Spirit. Can we do ours with less?

TELLING PEOPLE ABOUT GOD

Some studies show that people fear speaking in public and death more than anything else, and in that order. One wag commented that most funeral attendees would rather be in the casket than give the eulogy. I would add that the absolutely greatest fear for believers might be telling someone about Jesus. We worry about being misunderstood, or being rejected. We fear we don't know the right words on such a crucial topic as a person's eternal destiny.

The Spirit shines here. Saul, the first king of Israel, experienced the same feelings of fear and inadequacy we do, until he was promised power in 1 Samuel 10:6 and 10: *"The Spirit of the LORD will come upon you in power, and you will prophesy* with them; and you will be changed into a different person. ... When they arrived at Gibeah, a procession of prophets met him; the *Spirit of God came upon him in power, and he joined in their prophesying"* (emphasis added).

Three elements are involved here: the Spirit, power, and telling about God. That process applies to each believer today as well it did when Jesus told his disciples: "But you will receive power when the *Holy Spirit* comes on you; and you will be my *witnesses* in Jerusalem, and in all Judea and Samaria, and to the ends of the earth" (Acts 1:8, emphasis added). A little bit later, we will see the repeated connection in the book of Acts between the disciples being filled with the Spirit and telling people about Jesus. When we are filled, the Spirit just splashes out of us onto others.

God doesn't just give us a task we fear, he also provides the power we need to succeed in it, through the Spirit.

TRANSFORMATION

Now, let's go a little deeper in exploring the power the Spirit brings to our lives. Would you like to drive the Lotus, yet feel stuck in the Escort? Have you ever felt frustrated at your lack of spiritual progress? Has a bad habit defeated you too often? The Spirit brings to us a power that will change our very identity. Let's go back to a previous passage, about the impact of the Spirit on the life of Saul.

In 1 Samuel 10:6 we read what the prophet spoke to Saul, the anointed but fearful king: "The Spirit of the LORD will come upon you in power, and you will prophesy with them; and *you will be changed into a different person*" (emphasis added).

That transformation didn't come from Saul's moral fiber or resolve. The power of the Spirit changed him. That same transforming power touches us. Instead of despair, we can "overflow with hope" (Romans 15:13). Inner strength can become a trait, instead of a weakness (see Ephesians 3:16). In our next chapter we will explore this subject in more depth.

As I have noted, I didn't plan on this chapter. But I am glad I got to think about the Lotus once more. Best of all, spiritually, we can each drive it. Now, let's discover how being filled with the Spirit will make us into different people.

Chapter 4

Supernatural Power
to Grow

Back in January 1999, my mother's health had declined so much that she had to move in with my sister. That left behind the Long Beach, California, home that she and Dad had bought in 1954, and in which my sister Jane and I grew up. Forty-five years in one house accumulates a lot of stuff to go through, and the month of May arrived before we finished.

Mom had quite a green thumb, with many plants dispersed around the house and yard. I have never grown much attached to most plants; my feelings about apricot trees perhaps come the closest to an emotional bond, and then primarily for their fruit. For some reason, Sheila wanted a camellia plant in a half wine barrel from the backyard. I tried to talk her out of it, but couldn't. So I hauled it and its container seventy-five miles to our Temecula home.

We found a nice spot for it; at least I thought it was nice. Apparently, it didn't think so. Blossoms never became flowers, and brown death tipped the yellowish green leaves. We repotted it, fertilized it, and even moved the pot around a few times, but nothing caused it to thrive. Then Sheila suggested that *we* take it out of the pot and put it in the ground. I knew that her *we* meant *me,* and resisted—for quite some time. But the plant continued to do poorly, so I finally "bit the bullet" and put the camellia in the ground. Amazingly, that plant began to thrive. Blossoms set and became flowers. Brown leaf tips became lush green. Finally, it looked the way a camellia should look.

Our Christian lives may mirror the same struggle. We are alive, people recognize us as Christians, but we just don't thrive spiritually. Nobody gets excited looking at us, not even us. Why? I suggest that we haven't let the Spirit fill us. We are stuck in the pot. We have made a start, but we have stopped the growth process. We are still driving the Escort while the Lotus sits in the garage.

How do we start growing again? By letting the Spirit fill us and transform us. The two books that Paul wrote to the church in Corinth provide some gardening tips that connect growth and the Spirit. We all know that the Corinthian church had problems, which is why Paul wrote the letters. Sin abounded, from divisiveness to immorality to permissiveness to pride to immaturity. I found seventy-three references to some form of the word *spirit* in those books. Could it be that the Spirit provides the solution to sin and stagnant growth? I think so. Two passages provide the foundation for allowing the Spirit to help us grow in Christ.

Stuck in the Pot

Many times we get stuck in the pot and quit growing. Why? The pot just doesn't have the room we need to stretch out and grow. It limits our root formation. The firm boundaries constrict us. The pot doesn't hold enough soil to provide the nutrients we need to flourish. The Christians in Corinth experienced that stoppage in growth:

> Brothers, I could *not address you as spiritual but as worldly*—mere infants in Christ. I gave you milk, not solid food, for you were not yet ready for it. Indeed, you are still not ready. You are still worldly. For since there is jealousy and quarreling among you, are you not worldly? Are you not acting like mere men? (1 Corinthians 3:1–3, emphasis added).

Paul divided humanity into three groups: *Natural* people have no commitment to Christ and live life their own way. *Spiritual* Christians allow the Spirit to guide and control their lives. *Worldly* Christians hang onto the world with one hand while reaching for the Spirit with the other. They get stuck in the pot. The Corinthians were brothers and sisters in Christ, but not spiritual ones. They allowed their sinful natures to influence them too much.

I am convinced that our prime reason for not growing comes from not intentionally choosing to follow the Spirit. We may fear the degree of change required. We may want to hold onto some acts that we don't want to leave behind. Our desire for comfort may exceed our desire for growth. Growth requires Bible reading, prayer, behavior change, and that cost can seem too high. With all of these excuses, we just don't want to go where the Spirit wants to take us. We see that tension between worldly and spiritual believers in Galatians 5:16-17, 24:

> So I say, live by the Spirit, and you will not gratify the desires of the sinful nature. For the sinful nature desires what is contrary to the Spirit, and the Spirit what is contrary to the sinful nature. They are in conflict with each other, so that you do not do what you want. ... Those who belong to Christ Jesus have crucified the sinful nature with its passions and desires.

Have we made an intentional decision not to gratify our sinful nature? Or do we desire a little of the natural world, and a little of the spiritual world? When we try to grab onto both, we get stuck in the pot. Our roots don't have room to grow. The smaller amount of soil can't absorb as much water and nutrients. We haven't intentionally chosen to allow the Spirit to fill us. We hold back, and as a result we don't grow.

Breaking the Pot

For me, taking the camellia out of the pot was easy; that old half wine barrel almost fell apart on its own. But we sometimes cling to our pots. Their limits provide security, and moving beyond the safe confines of our comfortable pot can frighten us. We tend to fear the unknown, and letting the fire of the Spirit burn certainly means we lose control.

But when the Spirit fills us, the pot that once limited us explodes. We become free to grow, just like that camellia. Let's look at our main text, 2 Corinthians 3:17-18:

> Now the Lord is the Spirit, and where the Spirit of the Lord is, *there is freedom*. And we, who with unveiled faces all reflect the Lord's glory, are being transformed into his likeness with ever-increasing glory, which comes from the Lord, who is the Spirit (emphasis added).

Focus on that first sentence, the promise that the Spirit brings freedom. The more we allow the Spirit to fill us, the more freedom we experience. Let's not make the classic mistake of thinking we are free to do anything we want, that sin no longer matters. Rather, we are freed from the limits of the pot. We are not root bound. We no longer have limited soil resources with artificial limits on our growth. We can grow to be what God designed us to be.

In the same way that the camellia was transformed when removed from the pot, our lives also experience transformation. The Spirit shatters the pot, and we can grow. But where?

Identifying Our Growth Potential

About twenty years ago we purchased our current house, then just three years old, from the original owners. The developer had offered a cash prize for the best front yard landscape within six months of moving in. It was a nice bribe to increase the curb appeal of the new development. John, the original owner of the house, worked for a landscape supply company and was determined to win the contest. He bought materials at cost and filled the yard with them. He succeeded and won the competition.

But he made one mistake. He put in plants to look beautiful at their current size, never thinking of what they would grow into. Or, maybe he thought of it, but planned on selling the house before then. Five years after planting, the yard had become overgrown. We have taken out eight full-size trees and countless smaller bushes. Why? John worked short term, not long term.

As Christians, when we break our pot and plan the development of our lives, we need to identify our long-term growth potential. What should our "yard" look like at full growth? I recently changed the landscape for a ten-by-twenty-foot area at our front curb. I planted a nice flowering pear tree in the center, laid some used bricks down over part of it, and went shopping for some low-lying junipers to cover the rest of the ground. The plants I bought only reach about six inches in diameter now, but they will grow to six feet in diameter. Right now, the area looks a little sparse, but when they reach full size, they will cover the ground and give us a nice looking curb area.

What direction is your life growing? Have you thought about it? Let's see what direction the Spirit desires to take you. Let's go back to the last passage, but consider just the last verse:

> And we, who with unveiled faces all reflect the Lord's glory, are being *transformed into his likeness* with ever-increasing glory, which comes from the Lord, who is the Spirit (emphasis added).

What is our long-term spiritual growth goal? The Spirit wants to transform us so much that we reflect the likeness of Jesus. That intimidates me. I am content to be a good person. But the Spirit yearns for me to look like Jesus, to be holy. That is an entirely different goal.

When we become Christians, we don't just become *better* people, we become *different* people. We share a family likeness. That theme runs throughout the Bible. Let's explore just a few passages on this subject.

God chose that goal of family resemblance for us at our creation: "Then God said, 'Let us make man in our image, in our likeness'" (Genesis 1:26). God created us to look like him.

Predestination often brings confusion about how it works, but Paul makes the goal exceptionally clear: "For those God foreknew he also predestined to be conformed to the likeness of his Son" (Romans 8:29). Paul knew that we should grow into Christ-likeness. And, Jesus himself echoed that in Luke 6:40: "A student is not above his teacher, but everyone who is fully trained will be like his teacher." What goal does Jesus have in teaching us? To be like him.

In the Garden of Eden, God created us to reflect his own image and likeness. Like a bad mirror, sin warps that reflection. But the Spirit fills us so that we can regain the ability to accurately express the likeness of God. The word *Christian* means little Jesus. We come *to* him to become *like* him. We ask "What would Jesus do?" before we act. We live our lives to please him. The camellia's goal was to be physically healthy and vibrant. Our goal is to be spiritually healthy and vibrant. The camellia's method was to break the pot. Our method is to let the Spirit fill us.

But we must be careful not to wrongly define what it means to be in the likeness of Jesus. Perhaps this statement is too obvious, but being in the likeness of Jesus does not mean standing on the beach with outstretched arms and proclaiming, "I am God," as Hollywood actress Shirley MacLaine did several years ago. Only one God exists, in three Persons. No others can make that claim. We don't become God, as some cults today teach.

God himself made that point clear in Isaiah 44:6: "This is what the LORD says—Israel's King and Redeemer, the LORD Almighty: I am the first and I am the last; apart from me there is no God." God wasn't merely the first god who then created a plethora of other gods. Personally, I wouldn't want to be God— I know myself too well. I wouldn't put up with all of your problems very long, and I am sure you would be just as impatient with me.

But we can develop God's character. The same inner traits that drive his behavior can become ours. How? By allowing the Spirit to fill us, and God's character comes along with his Spirit:

"But the fruit of the Spirit is love, joy, peace, patience, kindness, goodness, faithfulness, gentleness and self-control" (Galatians 5:22-23).

We receive the Spirit when we come to Christ, we receive the fullness of the Spirit when we let him have full reign within us, and we receive the fruit of the Spirit as we allow him to transform us into the likeness of Jesus. But, on a practical level, how does this transformation take place?

God's Garden Tools of Transformation

Putting Mom's camellia in the ground only required a few simple tools: a shovel, some gloves, and a radio so I didn't have to whistle while I worked. The Spirit also provides three primary tools we can use to break our pots and freely grow. Let me suggest that you accept the Holy Spirit as the Master Gardener of your spiritual journey, one who knows the unique traits of each plant in the garden of your life, who knows the soil composition of your heart, who prunes perfectly your unfruitful branches, and who provides just the right fertilizer needed by each plant in each type of soil within you.

PLANT BARE ROOTS IN YOUR LIFE

Although I obsess over apricots, store-bought ones may be the most beautiful, expensive, and tasteless fruit offered in markets. So, after moving into our Temecula house, I prepared the soil in our side yard and went shopping. I had read that "bare root" trees developed best, and since our local nursery stocked them, I picked one up. I am not sure what I expected, but a three-foot twig with literal bare roots surprised me.

I properly planted it, and apricots have since blessed us. But the tree would never have grown if it hadn't been brought into intimate contact with the soil. Those bare roots needed to be surrounded by dirt to absorb the water, minerals, and nutrients necessary for growth.

We are the same way: in order to grow we need to be in intimate contact with God, and the Spirit provides that. Please forgive the following long passage from 1 Corinthians 2:9-16, but it demonstrates how being filled with the Spirit enhances our contact with God the Father:

> However, as it is written: "No eye has seen, no ear has heard, no mind has conceived what God has prepared for those who love him"—but God has revealed it to us by his Spirit.
>
> The Spirit searches all things, even the deep things of God. For who among men knows the thoughts of a man except the man's spirit within him? In the same way no one knows the thoughts of God except the Spirit of God. We have not received the spirit of the world but the Spirit who is from God, that we may understand what God has freely given us. This is what we speak, not in words taught us by human wisdom but in words taught by the Spirit, expressing spiritual truths in spiritual words. The man without the Spirit does not accept the things that come from the Spirit of God, for they are foolishness to him, and he cannot understand them, because they are spiritually discerned. The spiritual man makes judgments about all things, but he himself is not subject to any man's judgment:
>
> "For who has known the mind of the Lord that he may instruct him?" But we have the mind of Christ.

Now, let's look at the step-by-step process by which the Spirit builds intimacy with God the Father.

Step One: We see that God has plans for us that exceed our dreams. We can't begin to imagine what God desires for us as we grow and mature in him.

Step Two: God reveals those plans to us through the Spirit. We have seen some of God's plans for us: to become Christlike, to develop God's character, to have a unique and vital ministry.

The Spirit reveals those plans using both the written Word of God and his direct connection with us.

Step Three: The Spirit reveals God the Father to us. The Spirit searches the mind and heart of God. Since the Spirit fills us, we also have access to the mind of God. We can understand God, who he is, what he has already given to us, what he desires to give us, where he wants to take us.

Step Four: We develop the ability to understand spiritual things. As a gardening novice, I didn't understand much about bare root plants before I purchased and planted that apricot tree. But I now understand how they work, why bare root succeeds. I have planted other bare root trees and a number of bare root roses. Why? I now have a better understanding of gardening. When the Spirit fills us, we understand spiritual things better all the time. We begin to comprehend how God's love and justice balance one another. We begin to comprehend how one God can exist in three Persons. No, we don't *fully* understand all spiritual things, but they start to make more sense to us as we develop a sense of God's mind and heart from the Spirit.

Step Five: We become more spiritually discerning—we begin to evaluate the likely spiritual impact of various choices we make. We don't just look at the immediate benefits of our actions; we consider their consequences as well. Remember how John designed the yard for the immediate appearance without considering long-term growth? With the Spirit, we can see a little farther down the road that lies ahead of us.

Step Six: We avoid the sense of being judged critically by others, particularly by unbelievers. Why? Since we have access to the mind of Christ, we gain an improved understanding of what really matters. Appearances become less important. Our reputation with people takes second place to God's perception of us. Or, we get closer to God. We get to know his heart. We get planted in the soil of the Spirit.

Now let's explore the tools the Spirit uses to transform our lives.

TIME

Remember the low-lying junipers I planted in our parkway? Right now, they look pretty scrawny. Six-inch-diameter plants don't fully cover that ten-by-twenty foot area, even with nine of them. I planted them, I fertilize and water them, and now I wait. Plants take time to grow.

So do we. Although the age in which we live demands instant everything, spiritual growth doesn't happen that way. We begin growing right away, but sometimes that growth doesn't show on the outside for a while. Some goals just take time.

Well before we married, my wife came back into a dynamic relationship with Christ, and in her excitement began telling her friends. Then a coworker passed along a comment from someone else about her, "She may be a Christian, but she sure doesn't act like one!"

Sheila knew she had changed, and so she thought long about the remark. She concluded, "It may not all show on the outside yet, but it's real on the inside." Over the years, those interior changes clearly worked their way to the outside.

That's biblical. Christians do things that Christians shouldn't do, and we always will. But we should do fewer of them all the time.

Let's go back to 2 Corinthians 3:18: "And we, who with unveiled faces all reflect the Lord's glory, are being transformed into his likeness *with ever-increasing glory,* which comes from the Lord, who is the Spirit" (emphasis added).

The *New Revised Standard Version* uses the phrase, "from one degree of glory to another," and I like the way we are reminded that we don't grow completely, all at once. Like the junipers that slowly grow in my parkway, the Spirit takes us step by step along the journey to spiritual maturity. So, while we don't excuse imperfection, we realize that we need patience because our growth needs the tool of time.

PRUNING SHEARS

Once we come into contact with the soil and its nutrients, and as time passes, we begin to grow. Strangely, that growth can sometimes be a problem. Let's go back to our parkway land-scape. We chose a beautiful flowering plum tree as the center-piece. Yes, it was bare root. Then some neighborhood kids thought it would be a great pivot point to swing from, and in doing so snapped the tree off at the base. Only about six inches of the trunk remained.

I used the tool of time to see if the wounded plant would survive, and within a year the stump had became a beautiful bush. About a dozen shoots sprang up from the remains, but a tree it was not. So I grabbed the pruning clippers, identified the strongest shoot, and carefully removed all the others. Now, once again, it's a tree. I expect that with a little more time, it can even withstand our neighborhood kids.

The Spirit does the same thing in our lives: he prunes us for maximum growth. Jesus revealed one function of the Spirit in John 16:8: "When he comes, he will *convict the world of guilt* in regard to sin and righteousness and judgment" (emphasis added).

Did you ever do something wrong, or even *think* of doing something wrong, and suddenly feel a guilty twinge? That's the Spirit convicting you. I both hate and love that feeling. I hate it, because by it the Spirit lets me know that some things I do or would like to do are wrong. I love it, because the Spirit lets me know that some things I do or would like to do are wrong.

But how else can we grow, if we move away from God? The Spirit lets us know if our acts help or hinder our growth in Christ. So the Spirit fills us as we accept his direction. In so doing, we increase our intimacy with God.

Let's take this process a step further. Some pruning obvi-ously deals with sin, as Jesus said. But some pruning deals with more subtle issues. May I suggest that the good is the most effec-tive enemy of the best? When we cling to the good, even though the best is available, we miss the mark God has set for us.

My own life expresses that truth. Before my senior year in high school, I committed my life to "full-time Christian service," or to the professional ministry. Only my shallowness exceeded my sincerity. I entered a Christian college as a ministry major, but questions arose at the end of the first year, and I appropriately switched to become a history major. After I returned to God, the issue of the ministry returned, and I became a youth pastor.

The youth group grew, but I got burned, so I resigned my position and moved to Taos, New Mexico. I worked as a caretaker for an unused guest ranch, did some hotel management, and became a real estate broker. The church there nudged me back into the ministry, and not always gently. I became an associate minister, then the senior pastor of three churches. Each church grew as God worked in people's lives in each one. I developed great relationships with fellow pastors. The professional ministry was good.

But it wasn't the best, at least not for me. The Spirit used a number of tools to let me know that fact by leading me into a ministry of writing and teaching, which is what I have been doing ever since. Did I do well at being a pastor? Yes, but my gifts and personality match my current form of ministry much better. I needed those years of service as a pastor as a foundation for what I now do. The good or the best? The Spirit will lead us to the best, at God's best time. Do you have something in your life that's good, but not the best? If so, follow the leading of the Spirit; let him prune you, and then see what God has in store for you.

Chapter 5

Supernatural Power to Share

Some time ago, I received one of the multitudes of forwarded email jokes from a pastor friend, Dan DeWitt of Kansas. I howled when I read it:

> A congregation decided to have four worship services each Sunday: one for those new to the faith; another for those who liked traditional worship; one for those who had lost their faith and would like to get it back; and another for those who had a bad experience with church and were complaining about it.
>
> They've named the services Finders, Keepers, Losers, Weepers.

With more than twenty years in local church ministry and with different styles of worship, I related easily. After I calmed down, I went through my email address book and forwarded it to others in the ministry or who teach about it. I probably forward such messages five or six times a day. Rather than sending out each good one to everyone on my list, I carefully identify who will most likely enjoy each. These messages seem to be divided into four types: patriotic, thoughtful, faith affirming, and emotional.

You probably receive many forwarded email messages as well. Why do we pass them along? We like to share "good stuff" with those who don't know about it yet. That's innate. If we find a good restaurant, we know which friends to recommend it to, and which not to recommend it to. If we discover a new book, we know which friends will be interested in it and which ones won't. The same holds true if we come across a great vacation destination; we know those to whom it will appeal and those to whom it won't. The list goes on and on. The point is that we share with others what has brought us pleasure.

But the greatest source of pleasure in my life doesn't get passed on five or six times each day. I love God more than anything else. I spend much time each day writing about how to walk with him more closely. But I don't tell five or six people daily who don't know him.

I feel bad about that failure on my part, and I should. Obviously, practical reasons abound. Because of my work, I am not out where I can talk to that many new people each day. Many times we have to develop a relationship before we can share most effectively. Spirit-led timing plays a crucial role in this sensitive area of personal witnessing. But Acts 1:8 haunts me: "But you *will* receive power when the Holy Spirit comes on you; and you *will* be my witnesses in Jerusalem, and in all Judea and Samaria, and to the ends of the earth" (emphasis added).

Notice the strength of that word *will*. Jesus did not say, "you *may* receive power," or "on occasion you *may* witness." He said, "you *will* witness." When the Spirit fills us, we *will* witness about Jesus. But do we?

I have discovered a significant difference between the typical Christian life and the typical Spirit-filled life. I am haunted by this difference; perhaps you are as well. If so, join me on this exploration of how to use the filling of the Spirit to better tell people about God.

The Typical Christian Life

Most of us know we should witness more. We want to do so, but we rarely do. The Christian pollster George Barna reported these disturbing facts in December 2001. First, only in Pentecostal, Assembly of God, and non-denominational churches did a majority of members tell a non-Christian about Jesus within the past year. Second, despite their reputation for evangelism, only 40 percent of Baptist adult attendees shared their faith in that time period. I suspect that most of those did so only once or twice.

Yes, we know the Great Commission:

> Then Jesus came to them and said, "All authority in heaven and on earth has been given to me. Therefore go and make disciples of all nations, baptizing them in the name of the Father and of the Son and of the Holy Spirit, and teaching them to obey everything I have commanded you. And surely I am with you always, to the very end of the age" (Matthew 28:18–20).

To carry out that command, we hire trained church leaders, we support missionaries both at home and abroad, and we minister within our church. But we seldom tell unsaved people about Jesus personally. We all recognize that truth, and we all feel guilty about it, but our inertia and fear exceed our guilt.

Most of us find many excuses to avoid sharing our faith. Let's examine just four factors that keep us from being more effective witnesses for Christ.

OVEREMPHASIS ON BIBLE KNOWLEDGE

Wendell came to Christ after several years in the computer field. He fell deeply in love with God and yearned for everyone to experience the same joy he had discovered. Then he saw a television preacher speaking about prophecy, and he thought he had found the key to evangelistic effectiveness. He applied his engineer's mind to the mysteries of end times. He worked to balance his career and family with his passion for prophecy. When I visited his home, time-line charts had taken over his living room. Cross-references and explanations dropped down from them indicating where specific passages fit into the overall scheme.

He bubbled with joy, "Pastor, if people would just read these charts, they couldn't help but accept Christ. It's all here, and so clear!"

I make no claims to be a rocket scientist, but I did teach science for two years. I have a decent mind that leans to the analytical. But I was lost in the complexity. I knew Wendell for several years, and yet I never knew anyone who came to Christ because of his charts. Some, including family members, discounted Christianity when they saw him get lost in setting dates for the return of Jesus. I could be wrong, but I am convinced that he could have brought more people to Christ by just telling them about him, demonstrating his love, and serving them.

Wendell fell into the trap that many of us do: we tend to revere the Bible, perhaps too much. We accept it as the Word of God and the supreme authority for our Christian lives and the model for how our churches should operate. We love to learn more about it. But we can easily slip into "bibliolatry," worshipping the content of the Bible more than its purpose. Like Wendell, we can become so enthusiastic about a scriptural topic that it consumes our thoughts and time. And, in so doing, we miss out on our Spirit-empowered mission.

Let's go back to Acts 1: beginning in verse 1 we discover the context for verse 8, which we read before:

> On one occasion, while he [Jesus] was eating with them [his disciples], he gave them this command: "Do not leave Jerusalem, but wait for the gift my Father promised, which you have heard me speak about. For John baptized with water, but in a few days you will be baptized with the Holy Spirit."
>
> So when they met together, they asked him, "Lord, are you at this time going to *restore the kingdom to Israel?*"
>
> He said to them: "It is not for you to know the times or dates the Father has set by his own

authority. But you *will receive power when the Holy Spirit comes on you; and* you will be my witnesses in Jerusalem, and in all Judea and Samaria, and to the ends of the earth" (Acts 1:4–8, emphasis added).

The disciples got caught up in setting dates for the return of Christ, much like Wendell. In verse 6, they wanted to know when Jesus would restore the kingdom. Now, Jesus taught much about that subject. But the purpose of his end-times teaching was to build motivation for the mission. That mission was given in verse 8: to be witnesses. We could paraphrase Jesus' comments as, "You have a job to do. Don't worry about when I am coming back; just get people ready for my return."

Let's be careful that we don't focus so much on knowing the Bible that we don't tell people about it and the one to whom it points (see John 5:39–40).

IGNORANCE OF THE BIBLE

In the midst of preparing our sanctuary for Easter Sunday, Ken Warren walked over to me with his five-year-old granddaughter.

"Pastor Tim," he said, "Nicole has a question, and we didn't quite know how to answer it. Could you give it a shot?"

I bent down and asked, "How can I help you, young lady?"

She replied, "Who made God?"

Let's be honest, just saying, "Well, God has always been there, no one 'made' him," doesn't really satisfy a five-year-old, or most adults. We all want more. That question delves into the nature of God, his attributes, and the biblical support for each.

Sometimes we hesitate to share our faith because we fear we will be caught, that people will discover that we are not Bible scholars, or that we will say the wrong thing and turn them away from God forever. So, rather than fail, we keep quiet.

I have absolutely no clue how a computer chip works. But that didn't keep me from using one to write this book. We don't have to understand deep theology, either, in order to talk about

God. We just need one thing: his Spirit in us. That is what we should and can talk about.

I like the ease of witnessing revealed in the *New King James Version* of 1 Peter 3:15: "Always *be* ready to *give* a defense to everyone who asks you a reason for the hope that is in you."

What should we focus on? The hope within us. Of course, we would all love to be able to explain every difficult question in the Bible, but it is enough to tell people about the change that God has brought in our lives. If they ask a question we don't have a clue about, we can simply tell them so. But then we should add, "Let me do some research, and I'll get back to you."

FEAR AND EMBARRASSMENT

One church developed a cookie ministry in which fresh chocolate chip cookies were delivered to visitors from the previous Sunday. A new deliverer felt very uneasy, so the ministry leader encouraged him, "Maybe you could spend just a minute talking to God before you walk up to the house."

When the deliverers returned, this fellow came to the ministry leader and exulted, "It worked! The prayer really worked! I prayed they wouldn't be home, and they weren't!"

That fear of telling others about Christ existed in the first-century church as well, and even in a pastor. Paul mentored a young man named Timothy, trained him for ministry, and appointed him as the pastor of the church in Ephesus. But Timothy had a problem that Paul had to address: *"For God has not given us a spirit of timidity,* but of power and love and discipline. Therefore *do not be ashamed* of the testimony of our Lord or of me His prisoner, but join with me in suffering for the gospel according to the power of God"* (2 Timothy 1:7–8 NASB, emphasis added).

It seems that Timothy was retreating; fear and embarrassment seem to have afflicted him. Most of us can identify with that. We may have a simple fear of not knowing what to say. We may not want people to think that we have become a "religious fanatic" or "weirdo." We may fear rejection, of ourselves or the message we give.

But whatever the cause, fear causes us to shrink back. Even if we do go out to witness, we pray that nobody's home.

CHRISTIAN FRIENDS

Please don't misunderstand. Never has a Christian friend encouraged me *not* to share my faith. But I have to admit that my Christian and church relationships take up so much of my time and energy that I just don't *know* any nonbelievers. That situation makes it difficult to share with people with whom I have no relationship.

Many studies have shown that six years after becoming a Christian, most believers have no significant relationships with nonbelievers. Other studies indicate that many unchurched people would attend services if asked by a friend they trusted. But if we know few unbelievers, we can ask few unbelievers.

In a previous pastorate, our church offered Sunday morning worship and Sunday school, Sunday evening worship, and a midweek service. We soon discovered that most of those on Sunday evening came "to support the church" and attended all the other services as well. They had abundant opportunities to be spiritually fed, but that feeding took up almost all of their free time.

So we cancelled Sunday evening services and told the members to spend the time with their neighbors and friends. Did it work? In a church that averaged eighty-five in attendance, there were fifty decisions for Christ the next year. I can't help but think we found a link. Maybe if we freed people from some of our time demands upon them, they could build connections with the unchurched.

I have become friends with a non-Christian neighbor with whom I go fishing in the Sierras. Sometimes we must sacrifice to build relationships! We have had some excellent discussions on the drive and while walking the streams. We have talked about the struggles we face, about spiritual things, about "guy stuff."

Has he accepted Christ? Not yet, but I have had numerous opportunities to share my faith with him.

Can you identify with some of these reasons we avoid sharing? The Bible describes a different dynamic when we are filled with the Holy Spirit.

The Typical Spirit-Filled Life

Typically, we tend to associate the filling of the Spirit with the charismatic gifts. We have seen that while that manifestation may occur, it doesn't do so for all Christians. However, God wants all followers of Jesus to experience the filling. In researching all the times the Bible mentions the filling of the Spirit, I have been struck by two findings. First, references to being filled with the Holy Spirit fill the pages of the New Testament. We surveyed some of those references earlier in chapter 1. Second, the most common expression of the filling is telling people about God—not speaking in tongues, but using one's normal language to convey what God has done.

While I don't want to minimize the charismatic gifts, I do desire to maximize the primary purpose of being filled with the Spirit, which is passing on the message of God. Let's go back over some of the passages and see the abundant evidence for that link.

John the Baptist came to prepare people for the Messiah; the Scriptures reveal that he was filled with the Holy Spirit from birth (see Luke 1:15).

When Mary, then pregnant with Jesus, visited her cousin Elizabeth, the expectant mother of John, we read: "Elizabeth *was filled with the Holy Spirit. In a loud voice she exclaimed:* 'Blessed are you among women, and blessed is the child you will bear!'" (Luke 1:41–42, emphasis added).

At John's birth that same thing happened again: "His father Zechariah was *filled with the Holy Spirit and prophesied:* 'Praise be to the Lord, the God of Israel, because he has come and has redeemed his people'" (Luke 1:67–68, emphasis added). In this family, each spoke about God after being filled with his Spirit.

When his parents presented the infant Jesus at the temple for circumcision, they met Simeon, and that same pattern was repeated:

> Now there was a man in Jerusalem called Simeon, who was righteous and devout. He was waiting for the consolation of Israel, and *the Holy Spirit was upon him*. It had been *revealed to him by the Holy Spirit* that he would not die before he had seen the Lord's Christ. *Moved by the Spirit,* he went into the temple courts. When the parents brought in the child Jesus to do for him what the custom of the Law required, Simeon took him in his arms and *praised God, saying:*
>
> "Sovereign Lord, as you have promised, you now dismiss your servant in peace. For my eyes have seen your salvation, which you have prepared in the sight of all people, a light for revelation to the Gentiles and for glory to your people Israel" (Luke 2:25-32, emphasis added).

We have already looked at Acts 1:8, which links the Spirit's filling of the early disciples with their ability to be witnesses. Keep in mind that the English word *martyr* is derived from the original Greek word for *witness* which indicates that we witness with our life, if necessary.

That link between filling and witnessing flows throughout the book of Acts. Acts 2 records the birth of the church on the Day of Pentecost. Look at what happened in verse 4: "All of them were *filled with the Holy Spirit and began to speak* in other tongues as the Spirit enabled them" (emphasis added). After being filled, they spoke. What resulted? Verse 41 tells us: "Those who accepted his [Peter's] message were baptized, and about three thousand were added to their number that day." The Spirit filled the followers, they spoke, and people responded.

That pattern continued in Acts 4:8: "Then Peter, *filled with the Holy Spirit, said* to them: 'Rulers and elders of the people!'"

(emphasis added). Let's stay in that chapter to see how the entire church had the same experience: "After they prayed, the place where they were meeting was shaken. And they were *all filled with the Holy Spirit and spoke* the word of God boldly" (Acts 4:31, emphasis added).

In Acts chapter 6, the growth of the church led to delegating the food ministry. A prime job requirement was to be full of the Spirit:

> "Brothers, choose seven men from among you who are known to be *full of the Spirit* and wisdom. We will turn this responsibility over to them and will give our attention to prayer and the ministry of the word."

> This proposal pleased the whole group. They chose Stephen, a man *full of faith and of the Holy Spirit;* also Philip, Procorus, Nicanor, Timon, Parmenas, and Nicolas from Antioch, a convert to Judaism. They presented these men to the apostles, who prayed and laid their hands on them.

> *So the word of God spread.* The number of disciples in Jerusalem increased rapidly, and a large number of priests became obedient to the faith (Acts 6:3-7, emphasis added).

One of those chosen, Stephen, developed a marvelous ministry that aroused great opposition. After a trial that led to his stoning, we read: "But Stephen, *full of the Holy Spirit,* looked up to heaven and saw the glory of God, and Jesus standing at the right hand of God. 'Look,' *he said,* 'I see heaven open and the Son of Man standing at the right hand of God'" (Acts 7:55-56). Stephen faced death and found the courage to tell about Jesus from his fullness of the Spirit.

A fervent young Jew named Saul helped those who killed Stephen. God chose this same person, later known as Paul, to carry the message of Jesus to the non-Jewish world:

But the Lord said to Ananias, "Go! This man is my chosen instrument *to carry my name* before the Gentiles and their kings and before the people of Israel …

Then Ananias went to the house and entered it. Placing his hands on Saul, he said, "Brother Saul, the Lord—Jesus, who appeared to you on the road as you were coming here—has sent me so that you may see again and *be filled with the Holy Spirit*" (Acts 9:15, 17, emphasis added).

Paul turned the world upside down with his teaching, powered through being filled with the Spirit.

Two chapters later, a revival broke out in the city of Antioch, and the apostles in Jerusalem sent a man named Barnabas to investigate. What qualifications did he have for this ministry? "When he arrived and saw the evidence of the grace of God, he was glad and *encouraged them all* to remain true to the Lord with all their hearts. He was a good man, *full of the Holy Spirit* and faith, and a *great number of people were brought to the Lord*" (Acts 11:23-24, emphasis added).

Let's look at just one more example of how being filled leads to witnessing, once again in a corporate manner: "When the Gentiles heard this [that the Gospel was for non-Jews as well as Jews], they were glad and honored the word of the Lord; and all who were appointed for eternal life believed. The *word of the Lord spread* through the whole region" (Acts 13:48-49, emphasis added). What provided power for this effective ministry? "And the disciples *were filled with joy and with the Holy Spirit*" (Acts 13:52, emphasis added).

We just surveyed twelve different passages that link being filled with the Spirit and witnessing. Now let's compare two truths: (1) God wants all Christians to tell about Jesus. (2) God wants all Christians to be filled with the Spirit. And best of all, the second provides the ability to do the first. Clearly, being filled and telling about Jesus is the normal Christian life.

So, if we don't share our faith, does that mean we are not filled, or that we don't take advantage of the filling? Whichever, either condition can be remedied.

How Does It Work?

But how does the connection between the filling and witnessing work? Do we automatically tell people about Jesus if the Spirit fills us? Most of us would think not, so let's explore how filling links with speaking. Once we understand the process, we can implement it.

Mornings and evenings, our two cats spend time inside with us, both for "family time" and meals. But most of the time they live outside in the yard, or in the garage, or they just roam somewhere. Basically, they do as they please. So, to meet our obligations as "owners," we keep a large basin of water available for them in the garage, which they can access through our kitty door.

Since I am a practical guy, I fill the basin as close to the top as I can get in order to minimize trips from our kitchen sink to the garage workbench. But if I make a misstep, or if a cat gets underfoot as I carry the water, the water spills. Of course, I would never have to worry about spills if I didn't fill the basin to the rim.

Do you see the point? The more we fill our lives with the Spirit, the more we "splash out" when jostled by life. But not much will spill out if not much is in us. Think back to the obstacles we face in sharing our faith. The fullness of the Spirit helps us overcome them so that we are able to express what God has done within us.

Making It Work

I have found that I am much more apt to splash God on people when I rely on the four basic steps listed below.

BE FILLED

First, we need to have something inside. We have covered how to be filled, but before we can share what is in us, we need to fill our lives with God: with thoughts of him, with an awareness of his continual presence. We should regularly ask ourselves: "What would God want me to do in this situation? What attitude should I have toward this rude cashier? How should I respond to the driver who just cut me off?"

FOCUS ON THE MISSION

This second step takes the first step one stage further: Be aware of God. Also, be aware of God's mission for us: to be witnesses, to tell people about the hope within us, to continually be alert for opportunities to share our faith.

Simple things can provide that chance. When asked by a person how I'm doing, I sometimes respond, "Better than I deserve." That response has sparked more than one discussion on the grace of God. A waitress gave me too much change, so I handed it back to her. She said, "Not many do that anymore." I then said that as a Christian, it is just the right thing to do. A discussion in line to pay a traffic ticket led to topics like justice and absolute truth. While flying cross-country, I spent the time reading a John Grisham novel. The person next to me asked why I liked Grisham, and I explained that he has a marvelous gift for weaving spiritual decisions into a gripping story. We talked about several of those issues, and had a marvelous time.

We can be gracious as we talk about what is real to us. We don't have to force the issue, or insist that others agree with us. Our job is to tell. Their job is to accept or reject. But they can't accept it if we don't share it. So the more we bring up spiritual issues in a relevant fashion, the greater their chance to come to Christ. By the way, I have found that the prayer most likely to be answered is one asking God for a chance to tell someone about him that day. But once we pray that prayer, we need to be alert to the answer!

RELY ON SUPERNATURAL POWER

Sharing our faith typically produces fear, but being filled with the Spirit gives us supernatural power to overcome that fear. Remember Acts 1:8: *"But you will receive power when the Holy Spirit comes on you;* and you will be my witnesses" (emphasis added). Just as the Bible links the Spirit with speaking, it also links the Spirit with power.

During a televised interview I was asked how we get that transforming power of the Spirit. Without being too simplistic, I replied that if we have the Spirit, we have that power. We just need to be aware of it, and to place ourselves in a position in which our own power isn't enough.

Too often we don't experience supernatural power because we only attempt what we can accomplish with our own human power. Years ago I heard an encouraging statement that continues to change how I live: "If you want to see God's power, attempt something so difficult that it's certain to fail if God isn't in it."

Supernatural power resides in us. So let's attempt some witnessing that stretches our limits, which goes beyond what we think we can do. The Spirit just *waits* for us to try something we cannot do so he can step in and do what only he can do.

FOLLOW THE SPIRIT

Remember the dynamic of Acts 1:8: We receive the Spirit, then we receive power, and then we witness. Where? In Jerusalem, Judea, Samaria, and to the ends of the earth. In other words, wherever we go. We are to spread the message over the entire earth, transcending cultural and comfort barriers.

Don't hold anything back when God whispers to you. Let the Holy Spirit lead you wherever he desires.

The world watched the saga of Martin and Gracia Burnham, kidnapped Christian missionaries in the Philippines. After they had been captives for more than a year, the military attempted to free them, but both Martin and a Philippina nurse were killed. Gracia returned to Martin's hometown of Rose Hill, Kansas. A local man, Steve McRae, proposed that the townsfolk build a home for Gracia and her three children who had never owned one. People donated nearly everything; the costs to Gracia and her family totaled only $5,000.00 for a $175,000.00 home.

While tremendously appreciative of the house, Gracia had a concern. "I try to tell the kids, 'Don't let this grow on you. If God calls you to go somewhere and live in a hut, go. Let's not let this house be something that keeps us here if the Lord calls us on.'"

Doesn't she depict a marvelous willingness to follow the Spirit? And millions have heard the good news of Jesus because of their willingness to witness, even with their lives.

In the same way, we, too, need to witness. We need to look for opportunities to tell others about Christ.

Do you remember the classic line in the movie *Top Gun,* where Tom Cruise's character explains an act by saying, "I had the shot, and I took it." Pray for chances to share your faith with others. Rely upon God's power. Follow the leading of the Spirit. And when you have a shot, take it. Tell about your hope. Tell about what God has done in your life. Let the Spirit lovingly splash out of you onto those around you. You won't run out, since he will fill you again and again!

Chapter 6

Supernatural Power to Develop Individuality

Melissa's blond beauty stunned me, and I knew her ice princess demeanor had to conceal layered depths of personality. We met in a role-playing class in college back in the sixties, when not all courses focused on academics. The class encouraged us to open up to one another, and when Melissa and I finally went on a date, we spent much time talking.

I mentioned that I thought I was somewhat unique, and she responded, "No, you're not that different from most people."

I dropped her off early, and never asked her out again. At that point in my life, I had never received a worse insult.

Yes, all people share common needs, drives, and desires. The human condition doesn't change much from century to century. But we yearn to be individuals, to succeed, to become known, to craft our own unique persona. We don't want to get lost in the crush of the crowd. We yearn for a reason for our existence, why we as a specific individual have significance. We want others to distinguish us from the masses. So we strive to achieve individuality. We adapt our unique style of dress, our little quirks, our own personal manner of speech—all in order to stand out from others.

In the face of this innate need of ours for recognition and appreciation, only being filled with the Spirit will maximize our individuality. Let's see how that process works.

Losing Our Lives

Although we yearn to be unique, various influences seem to sap our individuality.

IN THE WORLD

The mere fact that billions of individuals exist at the same time makes us struggle to feel special. We walk through a crowded mall at Christmas, and our only significance to others is as an obstacle to get past to reach their next shop. Most of us never get noticed beyond our relatively small circle of friends, family, and coworkers.

Not only have we given up our childhood dreams of becoming President of the United States, we don't even know anyone who knows him. We are not known well enough even to get elected to the local school board. Most of us live in large cities and remain obscure.

Yet we want to think we are unique.

IN EASTERN MYSTICISM

A variety of forms of Eastern mysticism have invaded our cultural beliefs over the last thirty years. Reincarnation seems to offer enhanced individuality, proposing that we come back again and again to live life over and over. But for what purpose? According to Eastern thought, when we finally "get it right," we merely merge into the cosmic unconsciousness and lose all our individuality. So our extended existence as an individual merely leads to non-existence.

Yet we want to think we are unique.

IN CHRIST

But Jesus offers a paradox about our individuality in Matthew 10:39: "Whoever finds his life will lose it, and whoever loses his life for my sake will find it." Let me paraphrase that verse: "If you enhance your individuality for yourself, then you will never achieve your full potential; but if you lose yourself in me, you will become unique."

That statement doesn't particularly make sense. Yet the Holy Spirit within us can develop what we uniquely begin with, maximize it, and add spiritual gifts to the mix until we become the distinctive individual God originally desired, created, and planned us to be. Now, let's examine how God makes us matchless.

Uniquely Created

In 2002, a jury convicted David Westerfield of the kidnapping and murder of young Danielle van Dam. They said the forensic evidence presented overwhelming proof of his guilt. Investigators found hairs consistent with hers on the sheets in his master bedroom and in his motor home. They discovered her fingerprints on the wall next to the bed in his motor home. Drops of her blood were found on his sport coat. Criminologists said the odds of that blood belonging to anyone else were one in 670 quadrillion, which is the number 670 with fifteen zeroes after it.

How could the forensic scientists identify her hair, fingerprints, and blood so precisely? Because Danielle van Dam was one of a kind, a completely unique individual.

God uniquely created each of us. Recent news reports tell of a London high school that uses a retinal scanning device to charge students for their lunches. Retinas differ with each individual. We have already mentioned the DNA pattern unique to each individual. A supermarket in the Midwest now gives customers the option of "paying with a fingerprint," one linked to a specific account. It is hard to counterfeit a "live" fingerprint! Experts confirmed the continuing existence of terrorist leader Osama bin Laden in the fall of 2002, when they matched his voice on a tape to previous voice recordings.

How can human beings do such amazing things? Because God created each person as one of a kind.

Uniquely Developed

Not only do we begin as completely discrete individuals, the exclusive path we each take increases our distinctiveness. I matured late, back in junior high days, and often felt out of place. But that inadequacy changed my heart. Since then, I have had a deep concern for the underdog, the unaccepted. So I have gotten involved with supporting an orphanage in Mexico and with cooking meals for the homeless. That involvement expresses something deep within my emotional makeup. Everyone has something they are passionate about, something that touches their inner person, something that uniquely develops within them.

Each of us has a unique blend of natural abilities. Often as teenagers we think we can attempt anything and succeed, but we soon learn what we can do well, and what we can't do well. Our abilities qualify us for some careers and eliminate others. At one point I wanted to play guitar and be a lead singer in a rock band. But when I discovered I couldn't even tune my guitar, I had to give up that dream.

I knew twin brothers through elementary school, high school, and Boy Scouts. Even after knowing them many years I struggled to identify which was which—until they spoke, or interacted. Although they possessed identical genetic material, differences between their personalities marked them and led them to different paths of life. Each of us has a special blend of personality traits, from shy to outgoing, loud to quiet, introverted to extroverted, optimistic to pessimistic.

I usually got pretty good grades in school, except for physical education, where I never received an A. In our school a student had to be a "super jock" to get an A in a regular physical education class, but all those on a sports team got one almost automatically. Dad razzed me about not getting an A, so we bet five dollars that I could get one the next term. Although my sprint speed would barely qualify me to outrun a sick snail, I could keep running at my slow pace for a long time. So I joined the cross-country team, made the varsity, and we won our league championship. Not only did I win five dollars, I also made friends and had experiences that shaped my life.

I can identify many "coincidental" experiences that influenced me, and I am sure you can do the same. Although not every experience will dramatically change us, some will. No one has our experiences, our perspectives, our heart and personality.

What does all this mean? God first creates each of us as a totally unique individual. Then we develop even more distinctiveness through our emotions, our abilities, our personality, and our experiences. Those forces alone craft an exceptional individual. But God isn't done yet. The Spirit then steps in to increase our individuality.

Uniquely Gifted

As Christians, we are each given by the Holy Spirit one or more spiritual gifts. These gifts enhance our individuality. The more we allow the Spirit to lead and guide us, the more we can use these gifts, and the more significant and irreplaceable we become. We not only possess a created and developed personal identity, we also grow into a unique ministry identity.

EACH BELIEVER HAS ONE (OR MORE!)

The church in Corinth struggled in trying to understand and wisely use spiritual gifts, so Paul devoted three chapters to that subject. His goal: to teach the followers of Jesus how to follow the Spirit. He began the twelfth chapter of 1 Corinthians with that purpose in mind: "Now about spiritual gifts, brothers, I do not want you to be ignorant" (v. 1). In verses 7-11 he expanded on that subject:

> Now *to each one* the manifestation of the Spirit is given for the common good. To one there is given through the Spirit the message of wisdom, to another the message of knowledge by means of the same Spirit, to another faith by the same Spirit, to another gifts of healing by that one Spirit, to another miraculous powers, to another prophecy, to another distinguishing

between spirits, to another speaking in different kinds of tongues, and to still another the interpretation of tongues. All these are the work of one and the same Spirit, *and he gives them to each one,* just as he determines" (emphasis added).

Very simply, the Spirit gives every believer one or more spiritual gifts. What *kind* of gifts are given, in addition to the ones just mentioned? First Corinthians 12:28 adds apostles, teachers, workers of miracles, gifts of helping and administration. Romans 12:6–8 mixes in serving, encouraging, contributing, leading, and showing mercy. Ephesians 4:11 adds evangelists, pastors, and teachers. First Peter 4:11 contributes speaking, and verse 10 adds a catch-all, "faithfully administering God's grace in its various forms."

By my count, I find twenty-two different gifts; other people categorize them differently and get a slightly different number. Let's not get too absolute. The four major passages that list spiritual gifts all have different lists. So, I am not convinced that those twenty-two exhaust the gifts of the Spirit. And, I tend to think that the Spirit may gift us with a particular ability for a certain time, then give us different gifts at other times.

But to get back to our purpose here, spiritual gifts help increase our uniqueness. Gifts don't fit into a cookie-cutter mentality. We are not all the same according to 1 Corinthians 12:29–30 (NASB): "All are not apostles, are they? All are not prophets, are they? All are not teachers, are they? All are not *workers of* miracles, are they? All do not have gifts of healings, do they? All do not speak with tongues, do they? All do not interpret, do they?"

Obviously, not all believers are apostles, or prophets, or teachers, or miracle workers, or healers, or speakers in tongues or interpreters. Why? Because God wants us to be different. He created us differently. The Spirit gifts us differently.

Now, just *why* do we receive these gifts? To make a spiritual impact on others, to benefit the kingdom of God. We are not talking about our natural abilities, every individual has those. But we only find spiritual gifts in those with a spiritual relationship with God. Those gifts amplify our original distinctiveness and provide an absolutely irreplaceable ministry for each one of us. Make no mistake: the Spirit gifts us to minister. Remember, 1 Corinthians 12:7 tells us that gifts are "given for *the common good*" (emphasis added): not to bless ourselves or to increase our self-esteem, but to touch others for God's sake. Begin with how uniquely God has created us, continue with how uniquely we have each been developed, then blend in a unique set of spiritual gifts, and each Christian has an absolutely unique ministry that no one else can fulfill. Why? Because our ministry flows from our personality, our natural gifts, our experiences, our hearts, *and* our spiritual gifts.

Expressing Our Uniqueness

Does that understanding give us a hint of our significance, of the fact that each of us can do some things for God that no one else can do? So, to enhance our distinctiveness, we need to use the God-given gifts we have received. Think back to what Peter said in a previous passage: "Each one should use whatever gift he has received to serve others" (1 Peter 4:10). If God created, formed, and gifted us inimitably, then we enhance that uniqueness as we express it with our gifts for ministry.

But notice what Peter did not say. He did not tell us to *discover* our gifts, but rather to *use* them. Recent years have seen a growing interest in discovering spiritual gifts. Tests help identify them. But nowhere can we find a verse to support that quest, which leads to one of two conclusions: Either all believers intrinsically and surely know their individual gifts, or else knowing those gifts ranks lower than using them.

Do we all automatically know our gifts? Apparently not, if we have to take tests to discover them. Why take a test if we already know the answer? When I first learned about spiritual gifts, I didn't have a clue as to what mine might be. Now, more than thirty-odd years later, I am just beginning to get some idea.

But, as we allow the Spirit to fill us, as we follow his leading in ministry, we will *use* our gifts. Please allow me to share three basic principles about how we can express our distinctiveness by using our gifts.

FINDING OUR ARENA

Where and how do we use our gifts? In 1 Corinthians 12:4-6 the apostle Paul gives us some clues: "There are different kinds of gifts, but the same Spirit. There are different kinds of service, but the same Lord. There are different kinds of working, but the same God works all of them in all men."

Gifts come from the Spirit, the specific arena of ministry comes from Jesus, and the results come from the Father. What a marvelous cooperation of the Trinity. Each has a particular role in developing our unique ministry.

Each Christian receives gifts from the Spirit, but no one gets all the gifts. Those gifts received may include the ability to teach, lead, serve, or encourage.

Jesus gives us our arena of service, the specific place where we are to use our gifts. We may use our gift of teaching in working with children, in leading adult Sunday school, or in ministering on a university campus. We may use our gift of helping in the preparation of Communion, as a parking lot attendant, or as a volunteer in the church office.

The Father provides the results that flow from what we do. In 1 Corinthians 3:6-7 Paul makes that point clear: "I planted the seed, Apollos watered it, *but God made it grow.* So neither he who plants nor he who waters is anything, but only God, who makes things grow" (emphasis added).

Doesn't that take the pressure off of us? We use our gifts to the best of our ability, and God takes care of the results. So if we see great outward growth, we avoid the pride that says *we succeeded.* If we don't see great outward growth, we avoid the discouragement that says *we failed.* God calls us primarily to be faithful in serving.

Now, how can we best determine how to use our gifts, and perhaps discover what they are? I like the "Toad Kissing Principle": before we meet the handsome prince (or princess), we have to kiss a lot of toads. In other words, we serve, we minister, and we try a lot of different ministry tasks and arenas. Then we see which ones God seems to confirm and which ones others confirm and we begin to focus on those gifts.

We learn what we do best and what we don't do well. And sometimes, because of the critical needs of the body, we do something that may not be our primary gift, but because we can do it, we do it. Since we learn our gift by serving, we always need to know *why* we are doing what we do.

CLARIFYING OUR MOTIVES

We can easily look at our giftedness and inflate our importance to the kingdom of God. We do so most often when our gift mix combines some of the more public, up-front ones. We can develop a subtle spiritual pride that causes us to look down on those with the gifts that we think are less important. Although one purpose of the Spirit is to unite believers, too often the way we view spiritual gifts can bring division instead. That's why we need to carefully identify our motives for service to be sure they are correct.

Let's go back to 1 Corinthians 12:7: "Now to each one the manifestation of the Spirit is given *for the common good*" (emphasis added).

Of the four major passages detailing spiritual gifts, three of them explicitly state that the Spirit bestows gifts upon believers to be used to serve others. The other passage implicitly says the same.

So if we desire the Spirit to fill us, we need to use the Spirit's gifts as the Spirit desires. Doesn't that make sense? We don't minister for our benefit, to show our importance, to build our self-esteem. We use our gifts to benefit the body of Christ. Of course, we also benefit in many ways from that service to others. We see how God made us unique, and we rejoice. We see people come to Christ and start to grow spiritually, and we celebrate.

Whenever we minister, we should continually ask, "How can I bless others with what I do?" Then, we should do what we are shown.

Steve and his family visited a church known for its dynamic worship leader. As they celebrated Communion, the worship leader played his guitar and sang, lost in God. But Steve's ten-year-old daughter noticed, "Daddy, he's worshipping. I can see that. But he distracts us from worshipping God also."

Whatever we do, let's be sure we clarify our motive, and our impact. Is this the best we can do to glorify God and bless others? That decision can be difficult, since we can do the right act for the wrong reason, or the wrong act for the right reason. I think we can combat that danger as we use our individuality to bless others and honor God.

BOLDLY GOING WHERE NO ONE HAS GONE BEFORE

Remember, no one has our unique mix of DNA, abilities, personality, experiences, and gifts. So, our ministry is absolutely unique. Absolutely no one can ever duplicate the ministry that the Father and the Son and the Spirit have crafted for each one of us.

Let's go back to our original definition of being filled with the Spirit, which is to let God do whatever he wants with us. To assist in the process, we must not drag our heels. I must confess, sometimes my heels have dug furrows like the Grand Canyon as I have resisted following the Spirit's leading.

But can we discover any valid reason to resist the Spirit in his desire to fill and use us? If our gifts can help people avoid spiritual death in the hereafter and to grow into the abundant life in the here and now, why should we be halfway committed? Why should we quench the fire that the Spirit wants to spark within us?

In 1 Thessalonians 5:19 Paul encouraged us: "Do not put out the Spirit's fire." In other words, "Don't keep the Spirit from doing what he desires by not fully receiving and using his gifts to you. Be bold. Be adventurous in your ministry. Try difficult tasks beyond your abilities, so that you may truly see what God can do in you. Take some risks."

I spent seven years serving as a pastor in San Pedro/Rancho Palos Verdes, California. Just before I left, I learned that the largest and fastest growing Protestant church in town had total cash reserves equal to one and one-half weeks of their budget needs. That is foolhardy. It is risky. It is definitely not prudent. But that church touched more people more effectively than any other church in town. Others had great reserves, but that church had great ministry.

May we do the same with the ministry God has designed for us. And as we do so, we will discover our uniqueness, our significance, the way in which we truly are one of a kind. The Spirit does good work when we let him. Let's let him do so.

Chapter 7

Supernatural Power to Develop Integrity

I have always loved the game of football, and even more to play than to watch. So, at the age of fifty-four, I joined our church's flag football league. I had been working out some and thought I was in decent condition. The first game, only five players showed up for our five-man team, so I was slotted to play both wide receiver and defensive back. For non-football fans, that means I had to do a lot of sprinting and changing directions Keep in mind; I am not a speedy guy. With me it is slow and steady, but our team needed help in that position—which means that we really needed help.

I enjoyed playing, and I did pretty well. I caught six passes that led to two touchdowns, and I would have scored if I hadn't been so slow. I caught one pass beyond the defenders and began lumbering toward the end zone, but a much quicker defender caught up to me. And, I didn't give up a touchdown on defense. That achievement may have been more luck than skill; a good quarterback could have shredded me.

But I paid a high price for that one hour of joy. My muscles throbbed with pain the entire next week. I swallowed aspirin and lived in our hot tub, but by the next Saturday I still moved gingerly. Even a thorough warm up and stretching exercises didn't loosen up those stiff and painful muscles.

Late in the first quarter, I went out for a pass. Just as I got past my man, he kicked me hard, in my lower calf, a rotten thing to do in a church league. But as I writhed on the ground, I realized he couldn't have kicked me; he wasn't close enough. Later, in the emergency room, the doctor confirmed what I had already suspected: my Achilles tendon had torn badly, nearly enough for surgery. After a good bout of physical therapy and many months of rest, it was *almost* back to normal.

I came face to face with a hard truth: a fifty-four-year-old body doesn't function as it did at forty-four, let alone twenty-four. Truth can be tough to face, particularly truth about ourselves. Mark Twain knew that well, "We do not deal much in facts when we are contemplating ourselves."

We frequently resist the hard edge of truth. But we cannot be filled with the Spirit without a willingness to fully embrace the truth (we call it integrity), and to live by the truth. Why? Think about what Jesus said in John 16:13: "But when he, *the Spirit of truth,* comes, he will *guide you into all truth*" (emphasis added).

First, look at his name—the Spirit of truth. Truth expresses his character. We cannot partake of the Spirit without a willingness to partake of truth. Following God requires a desire to become more like him in character. Since truth describes the Spirit, we need an eagerness for truth if we claim an eagerness for God.

Second, look at his function—to guide us into *all* truth, not just some, but all. How can the Spirit fill us if we won't go where he wants to take us? Many of us make it impossible for the Spirit to fill us because we don't possess a desire to walk in the truth. When we resist truth, we resist the Spirit.

We cannot have integrity without a commitment to truth. Integrity requires that we accept the truth and strive to live in it consistently. Obviously, we can't do that perfectly; we are human and prone to fail. But this desire for integrity and truth needs to become a guiding value for our lives. When we fail, we need to acknowledge our failure and get back on track. We need to listen to those who speak the truth to us about our lives.

For this chapter, imagine truth as a rock, the bedrock foundation for life. Because truth possesses that hard edge, if we fall on a rock, or get hit by one, we can get hurt. But when we build on a rock, we can construct a life that lasts. Let's explore how integrity develops as we allow the Spirit of truth to fill us.

Caught Between a Rock and a Hard Place

Have you ever been stuck between two options, neither of which seemed very attractive? Truth can put us in that dilemma, and a couple in the early church experienced it. Many believers sold properties and gave the profits to the apostles to meet the needs of church members. Ananias and Sapphira yearned for the admiration these people received, but found it hard to sacrifice as they had done. So the two of them put their heads together and agreed on a plan.

They also sold some property, but they kept part of the proceeds, and gave away the rest to the leaders, pretending to give it all. The operative word here is *pretending*. Peter properly saw the significance of their attitude and actions as recorded in Acts 5:3-5:

> Then Peter said, "Ananias, how is it that Satan has so filled your heart that you have *lied to the Holy Spirit* and have kept for yourself some of the money you received for the land? Didn't it belong to you before it was sold? And after it was sold, wasn't the money at your disposal? What made you think of doing such a thing? You have not lied to men but to God."
>
> When Ananias heard this, he fell down and died (emphasis added).

The rock? People didn't view Ananias and Sapphira as spiritually deep and willing to sacrifice. The hard place? To change that perception, they had to knowingly and intentionally lie. They violated the truth, and that rock crushed them.

Does that mean that if we *ever* lie, in even the smallest way, we will be struck dead? I am living proof that such a dire consequence doesn't always happen. I suspect you are too. But let's not minimize the hazard of lying, just because we don't instantly get treated like Ananias and Sapphira.

Let me suggest that being filled with the Spirit requires that we choose between the full truth and anything less. Following are some examples of the devices we often use to avoid telling the full truth.

OUTRIGHT LIES

Many of us have used this device, perhaps on our income taxes. We don't always report all of our income, or we exaggerate our deductions. Then we sign the return that says all the information in it is accurate. We rationalize that what we do really is okay, but we know it's not.

PARTIAL TRUTHS

These untruths knowingly mislead. We leave out significant information that gives the wrong impression, and we justify doing so since we didn't directly lie. But we intended to deceive. We are late coming home from work, and our wife wonders what took us so long. So we smile and bring out the flowers from behind our back, and she melts. We don't mention the hour we spent somewhere doing something we shouldn't have, or the fact that we picked up the flowers from a vendor on a street corner. But we rationalize our actions by telling ourselves that we didn't "flat out lie."

WHITE LIES

These little "mistruths" shade the truth enough to make others feel better, or to make ourselves look better. For example, we may tell our wife she looks great in a certain dress although we know better and just don't want to deal with her hurt feelings. Or we may "slightly exaggerate" something about us. I love the line, "The older I get, the better I was."

Choosing truth means that we have to make some tough choices, as when we are "caught between a rock and a hard place." Telling the truth may damage us or others, but telling less than the truth damages our closeness with the Spirit. How do we deal with being forced to choose between two difficult options?

Let's get to the heart of it. We look at our options, and we consistently choose to do what we most want to do. We may face an Ananias and Sapphira decision: do we want others to think well of us or do we want the Spirit to think well of us? We may face an economic decision: do we falsify our tax return, or do we cling to the Spirit of truth? Behind these decisions is the basic fact that the truth sometimes hurts.

We will only choose truth when we desire intimacy with the Spirit more than we desire the alternatives: our reputation, our economics, our comfort, our peace. At least for me, that picture clarifies things. I can easily *say* I want the Spirit most, but my choices *show* what I really want most. For me, I need the stark truth of remembering that if I lie, I hurt my closeness with God. I have to ask myself, am I willing to take that risk?

Make no mistake, I don't always make the right choice. (I had to put in this confession, since my wife will read these words.) But I find that those hard choices become easier to make when I remind myself that choosing the option of less than full truth carries a heavy price tag. Does that make sense? If it does, then the next step is logical.

Hug a Rock

Some years ago, the "pet rock" craze hit the American scene. As pets, rocks have some real benefits. You don't need to feed them. You don't need to water them. You certainly don't have to follow them around with a pooper-scooper and pick up after them. You can leave them alone while you are on vacation without arranging for someone to look in on them. And when you return, they don't pout and punish you for hours for leaving them. (Warning: only cat owners will understand that advantage.) Even so, few pet rock owners truly loved their pets.

But followers of Jesus need to both love and hug a rock. Does that sound strange? If we truly desire the Spirit of truth to fill us, and if rock symbolizes truth, then we need to hug a rock, to love a rock—that is, the rock of truth. We need to embrace full truth, regardless of the costs and difficulties.

Let's expand on this thought. To be a Christian means to know God personally and deeply. God exists in three equal persons: the Father, the Son, and the Holy Spirit. The Bible refers to each of them as Truth.

In Psalm 31:5 David described God the Father that way when he wrote: "Into your hands I commit my spirit; redeem me, O LORD, *the God of truth*" (emphasis added).

Jesus described himself that way in John 14:6: *"I am* the way and *the truth* and the life. No one comes to the Father except through me" (emphasis added).

Jesus also described the Holy Spirit with that term in a verse we looked at earlier, John 16:13: "But when he, *the Spirit of truth,* comes, he will guide you into all truth" (emphasis added).

Not only can we know this God of truth, we can become like him. The Spirit transforms us into the character of God: "And we, who with unveiled faces all reflect the Lord's glory, are being *transformed into his likeness* with ever-increasing glory, which comes from the Lord, who is the Spirit" (2 Corinthians 3:18, emphasis added). Now, if truth expresses an integral part of God's identity, then truth certainly should become part of our identity as we know and grow in his likeness.

That attribute of God particularly applies to our relationship with the Spirit. We have already seen that all followers of Jesus receive the Spirit (see Acts 2:38). We have seen that the normal Christian life means that the Spirit fills us (see Ephesians 5:18). And Jesus linked our connection with the Spirit and truth in John 14:16–17, "And I will ask the Father, and he will give you another Counselor to be with you forever—*the Spirit of truth.* The world cannot accept him, because it neither sees him nor knows him. But you know him, for he lives with you and will be in you" (emphasis added).

In this passage Jesus described the close relationship that believers have with the Spirit. First, he is *with* us; that's connection. But the connection gets more intense. Jesus also said that the Spirit lives *within* us. We can *know* him, and in biblical language the word *know* also refers to sexual intercourse. That is intimacy.

So, think with me. If we desire a close relationship with this type of being, then we need a desire to have that same character trait of truth within us. When we resist truth, we resist the Spirit. When we move away from truth, we move away from the Spirit. Why? Because the Spirit is truth.

By their behavior, Ananias and Sapphira demonstrated that they loved popularity more than integrity. They truly didn't desire a relationship with the Spirit if it required scrupulous honesty and integrity. They didn't want to hug a rock.

A partial commitment to truth prohibits the Spirit of truth from filling us.

Be a Rock Hound

Our church in Temecula included several rock collectors. They would invade the desert even during the hottest days of summer looking for "attractive" rocks. They would then bring promising ones home, polish them and slice them, and we would admire their beauty. One of these rock collectors, Lou Fritts, described himself as a "rock hound," and I naively asked what that meant.

"When you go out looking for rocks, you put a handful of marbles in your pocket. Whenever you pick up a rock, you replace it with a marble. When you've lost all your marbles, you're a rock hound."

We may feel that we have lost our marbles if we choose to pursue truth and forsake untruth, especially when we think about the degree of truth we need to seek. Let's refer to what Jesus said in John 16:13:"But when he, the Spirit of truth, comes, he will guide you into *all truth*" (emphasis added).

What did Jesus mean by that phrase "all truth?" I used to think that he meant that the Holy Spirit would guide me into all the truth about God and the Bible that I needed to know. I didn't go nearly far enough in my definition of truth. If I yearn to be filled with the Spirit of truth, who wants to guide me into all the truth, then I can't place limits on the truth I seek. That fact frightens me.

I need to seek the truth about *myself:* my weak spots, the areas of myself in which I am vulnerable. Only when I recognize and acknowledge them can I build a strategy to avoid direct hits and develop some strength in those vital areas.

I need to seek the truth about the sins I have committed, the ways I have wronged people. I need to acknowledge my sins, ask forgiveness, and make restitution when possible. Most of the time my weak ego would prefer to ignore these proofs of my humanity.

I need to seek the truth about temptations. I need to recognize and acknowledge that some issues have spiritual significance and are not just personal quirks.

I need to seek the truth about my gifts and abilities. If I can ignore them, then I won't have to step out and use them. I can stay where I am comfortable. But if I acknowledge that God has gifted me in a certain area, then I am responsible to take the next step.

I need to seek the truth about *others* so I can build honest relationships with them. I need to acknowledge their strengths, and let them do some things they do better than I. My weak ego would rather not admit that anyone can do anything better than I, but that's not true. I need to acknowledge their weaknesses—and help them avoid needless failure. Sometimes I would rather make excuses for them and not have to get involved. I would rather see their best and not have to deal with their difficulties.

I need to seek the truth about our *culture.* What values do I encounter that are contrary to those of God? And, what cultural values that I don't like are just my personal preference and don't represent kingdom values? I dislike rap music as much as my parents disliked rock and roll, but is the style itself a problem, or is it just some of the lyrics?

I need to seek the truth about how changes in the culture affect the way I best minister to it. Part of me would prefer to do what I have done before, what has worked in the past. That is easier than revamping my style of ministry. I need to seek the truth about new ways that work well at influencing people for Christ.

I am fifty-five years old as I write this, and I can get the senior discount at many places. But I don't want to minister just to those in my generation and the generation before it. I received one of my best compliments some time ago, when I met the man who edited one of my recent books. After an hour or so, he acknowledged, "Tim, I have to tell you, I was surprised when I saw you. From your writing style, I expected someone much younger."

That transition in writing style took work. My natural bent is to write heavy in content and light in story. But that style doesn't communicate as effectively as it did thirty years ago, and I need to face that truth and adapt my style to it.

And, I need to seek the truth about the *kingdom of God*. Long ago I heard a great definition of total commitment to God: giving all I know of myself to all I know of God. Doesn't that definition require a continual search for more truth about both me and God? I have learned that God cares about the tone of my voice when I deal with the bank employee who made a mistake that bounced six checks and brought fees of $120.00. I didn't know that before!

I need to seek more of the truth about the Person of God. Right now I am reading through the Gospels specifically to get a feel for the type of Person Jesus is and was. Why did he react to people the way he did? Why did he teach certain things? Why did he heal people? Why did he soundly condemn religious hypocrites? I am learning a lot of truth about the friend I have known pretty much my whole life.

Seeking the truth may mean disruption in our lives. We must be willing to leave the security of what we know and risk the changes that greater truth will bring. That prospect stretches us, but if we yearn for the Spirit of truth to fill us, we need to follow wherever the truth leads. As disruptive as that journey can be, the destination rewards us amply.

Jesus cared a lot about truth; we have seen that fact in some of the quotes from him about the Spirit found in the

Gospel of John. Here is one more, in John 8:32: "Then you will know the truth, and the truth will set you free."

Seeking full truth frees us from the slavery of lies. It frees us from the bondage of partial truth. It frees us so the Spirit can do with us what he desires. And I have experienced the joy that comes when we seek the truth in the midst of difficult times.

I shared in a previous book how my wife and I went through some very difficult marriage times. Questions and doubts overwhelmed me. Would we make it through? Should we? Wouldn't it be easier just to give up and start over? Wasn't there someone out there who would love me as I thought I needed to be loved? Wasn't there someone out there who wanted to be loved by me? I knew that not all these questions were good, but each one pressed in on me. Each possible answer proved as elusive as a cloud of smoke drifting in the air.

But during all that uncertainty, I clung to several rocks that I knew were true. I knew for a fact that God cared about both Sheila and me. I knew he had brought us together. I knew he had already worked to keep us together. I knew he wanted us to have a healthy marriage, and that if we both cooperated, we could have it. I knew I wanted that kind of relationship, and I knew Sheila wanted it too.

Those rocks built the foundation of hope, reconciliation, restoration, and health. But I would have found it almost impossible to build health into our marriage if I had not held onto what I knew was true. As Sheila and I both did so, we found the freedom that truth brings.

Throw Some Rocks

Back when I was about eight, some of us neighborhood kids were playing hopscotch on the front sidewalk. I had been using a small rock as a "lagger," to mark the right box. When we finished the game, I bent down, scooped up the rock, and in one motion tossed it into the street. Unfortunately, a car drove by just then, and I heard the rock hit it. Next I heard the car's brakes go on, and I ran—stupidly, into my own backyard. Soon Dad came out with the driver of the car, and I learned the consequences of throwing rocks!

But let me suggest that we *should* throw rocks, when rocks represent truth, according to Ephesians 4:25: "Therefore each of you must put off falsehood and speak truthfully to his neighbor, for we are all members of one body."

When we commit to full honesty, one of the most important areas we must deal with is that of speaking truth. Why? When we express truth, we express the Spirit's character. As we do so, he fills us, and we can follow his leading.

But notice the specific reason given in that verse. We should speak honestly to one another because we are all members of the same body. If I stub my little toe, that impact affects my entire body. I limp, I move slowly, and I can't do some things. Why? My little toe is connected to the rest of my body. I can't hide the truth from myself, at least, not for long, even when I try.

So if we want the Spirit to fill us, we need to be sure that everything we speak is true. Therefore, *before* we speak, we should ask ourselves, "Am I sure this is true?" Only when a thought passes that honesty test should it pass our lips. Sometimes I think something *probably* is true, but that is not good enough. As Christians, we need a scrupulous commitment to say only what we are sure is true.

Can we sometimes *not* throw rocks? Do exceptions exist? Of course. We can validly not share information, as long as we don't deceive others by so doing. Private information deals with issues that others have no need to know. Other information can bring damage if it were broadcast. Some information is safe with some people, and not with others. We should use discretion and good judgment with our commitment to tell the truth. But I fear our mistakes usually deal with not being truthful enough rather than being too truthful.

In our efforts to be honest and truthful, let's not get so legalistic that we can't have fun with practical jokes and humorous exaggeration in those times when people don't expect us to tell the truth. One man won a tall tale contest by saying that in his home he had three flashlights and two sons, and they all worked, which, of course, is absolutely impossible! But we can discover truth before we say it fairly easily. The difficulty comes with the next stage.

Throw those Rocks Softly

Did I need to throw that rock away? Yes. Did I need to carelessly throw it where I did? No. So we need to throw the rocks of truth, but we need to throw them with great care. Remember, the truth can hurt, and we should avoid inflicting needless damage.

Some people take great pride in being honest: "You always know where you stand with me. I just tell it like it is, and if people don't like it, that's their problem." We can easily think truthfulness allows abusiveness. Yes, we need to speak the truth—the whole truth—and to avoid partial truth and white lies. But look how the Spirit encourages us to do that in Ephesians 4:15: "Instead, *speaking the truth in love, we will in* all things grow up into him who is the Head, that is, Christ" (emphasis added).

We grow in spiritual maturity as we speak the truth. But we don't do it recklessly, we do it in love. Love means acting in the best interests of the person we love. So we need to craft our speech to run it through the filter of honesty, then through the filter of love. That sounds so easy, as when the Beatles sang, "All we need is love." However, most of us struggle with knowing the loving words to say and the loving thing to do. Most of us don't have a Ph.D. in love, and so we need some help in knowing what to say and do. Just a few verses later, we get a lesson on love language:

> In your anger do not sin: Do not let the sun go down while you are still angry, and do not give the devil a foothold. ...
>
> Do not let any unwholesome talk come out of your mouths, but only what is helpful for building others up according to their needs, that

it may benefit those who listen. And do not grieve the Holy Spirit of God, with whom you were sealed for the day of redemption. Get rid of all bitterness, rage and anger, brawling and slander, along with every form of malice. Be kind and compassionate to one another, forgiving each other, just as in Christ God forgave you" (Ephesians 4:26–27, 29–32).

Right in the middle of practical insights on how to express love in our speech, we find the encouragement in verse 30, "Do not grieve the Holy Spirit." Doesn't that suggest our theme of allowing the Spirit to fill us so that we don't work against what the Spirit desires to do in our lives? The Spirit can fill us when we lovingly speak the truth as described here. But how do we express truth?

First, we *control our anger* when we speak (see verse 26). In the original language that statement is a command: "Be angry, but don't sin." We can get angry. Sometimes anger expresses a love for God and others, a hatred of injustice and pain. But we cannot let it run out of control, we cannot say things in anger that we don't mean or that cause damage. We must deal with issues quickly, not allowing the anger to fester. We cannot keep telling people how wronged we were.

Second, in verse 29, our loving language must *build up others* and bring grace into their lives. We must ask ourselves, "How can what I say, and how I phrase it, benefit others?" If we can't see a benefit to them, we must remain silent. We must always speak in love. Sometimes our loving truth will bring pain that is necessary to heal a wound or to bring awareness of a situation that needs to be confronted, dealt with, and resolved. Building others up doesn't mean that we must always avoid causing pain, just that the pain we cause must always lead to health.

Third, verse 31 gives us a huge list of *heart attitudes to avoid*, things like bitterness, rage, and anger. Most of us find it hard to express words of love when bitterness rules our hearts. We can't really express love and rage simultaneously. So we must check our attitudes before we speak. We must ask ourselves whether we will minimize our bitterness by saying things that add to other people's burdens.

Fourth, we must offer loving words of forgiveness (see verse 32). Forgiveness provides the key to our last point. When others wound us, we hurt. We want to wound back, to get even, to make them feel what we are feeling. As bitterness grows, anger settles in, and we want to rage at them. Forgiveness short-circuits all that flow of negative energy. When we feel the temptation to strike back, we must quietly remind ourselves that we have to forgive others of their sins against us just as God has forgiven us of our sins against him. We must re-program our minds to think and speak as he does.

Now, when we take these four steps to speak the truth in love, we open ourselves for the Spirit to fill us. When we don't speak in love, we grieve the Spirit and hinder what he desires to do in us.

Life on the Rocks

We usually think of a "life on the rocks" as a life that is going through hard times. In the context of this book, life on the rocks means living in the truth; desiring to increase the amount of truth available in life, not decrease it; building each dimension of life on the truth.

In Psalm 15:1–5 we find a marvelous example of a life on the rocks, a life with integrity, a life that allows the fullness of God:

> LORD, who may dwell in your sanctuary? Who may live on your holy hill?
>
> He whose walk is blameless and who does what is righteous, who speaks the truth from his heart and has no slander on his tongue, who does his neighbor no wrong and casts no slur on his fellowman, who despises a vile man but honors those who fear the LORD, who keeps his oath even when it hurts, who lends his money

without usury and does not accept a bribe
against the innocent.

He who does these things will never be shaken.

Let's begin by mentioning the goal in verse 1, intimacy with God. We will come back to this context in the next section, but keep it in mind. How do we get there? David mentions four steps that describe how to build a life of integrity that pleases the Spirit.

First, he combines walking blamelessly, doing what is righteous, and speaking the truth. Overall, that means living in accord with God's truth, and when we don't live that way, admitting it. I know that's hard to do, but walking without blame doesn't mean that we never sin, just that we acknowledge the truth of our sin because our heart desires to live out God's truth.

Second, David links doing good to others with our language, meaning that we don't slander or slur others. Doesn't that sound like Ephesians 4:29? Our Spirit-led words will build others up; they won't be negative and tear people down or damage their reputations.

Third, the psalmist suggests that as Spirit-filled Christians we keep our word, even when it hurts. That's integrity, making our actions match our words, not making promises we won't keep.

Fourth, David indicates that we have financial integrity; we don't take advantage of people; we pay our bills.

Those standards stretch us, don't they? They give us a clue why a commitment to truth will challenge us and change our lives. But let's go back to the goal of this passage, the goal of our chapter.

When Rocks Give Comfort

Not long ago, I went with a group of men up to Big Pine Creek in California's Sierra Nevada mountains. Three of us hiked into the back country for some wild trout fishing, part of a trip that six of us had taken thirty years earlier. We had backpacked in a day and a half and experienced some majestically pristine wilderness. We got to our first night's camping spot, a beautiful meadow near actor Lon Chaney's old cabin.

But spring hadn't left the mountains, and the meadow was quite boggy. Then we found a huge rock, probably six feet high, twenty feet long, ten feet wide, and flat on top. We slept on it that night, nice and dry. I was amazed at the comfort a rock could give!

The rocks of truth also bring comfort to us. Let's go back to that first verse in Psalm 15:1: "LORD, who may dwell in your sanctuary? Who may live on your holy hill?" These terms describe intimacy with God, the equivalent of being Spirit filled. David answered these questions by describing a follower of God who lives in truth and integrity.

What nugget can we find in these verses? We can only be filled with the Spirit of truth when we commit ourselves to the truth, when we speak the truth in love, and when we live in the truth. Walking in truth opens our lives for the Spirit to take us where he will. May we allow nothing in our lives that might grieve the Spirit of truth.

Chapter 8

Supernatural Power to Achieve Significance

At the beginning of my senior year in college, I had taken or registered for all of my required courses. Since I had an opening for an elective, I checked the time slots that fit my schedule and saw a class titled Beginning Acting. I had been in a few church dramas (and I owned a bathrobe), so I signed up. I wasn't very good at that kind of thing, but I enjoyed it. Perhaps, way down deep, I hoped to get "discovered" and become a famous actor.

At that time Pepperdine University which I was attending produced two major dramas each year, and the teacher encouraged those in the acting class to try out. I picked out a very minor role for our spring play, *You Can't Take It with You,* and prayed a lot. While walking to the tryouts with a friend, he asked what role I wanted to audition for, and I mentioned my desired bit role. He said I ought to try out for the role of Tony Kirby, the male romantic lead. He also said that the odds-on favorite for the female romantic lead, Alice Sycamore, was a coed named Pam, one of the prettiest girls on campus. I couldn't resist. I knew I didn't have a shot at the part, but I tried out for both roles. The director had a callback, and he asked me to read again for Tony. I got the role, and in the play, I got the girl.

I had a ball doing *You Can't Take It With You.* In that play, two very opposite families are brought together by their children who get engaged. The Kirbys are driven, ambitious, and successful. Their philosophy is that you must work long and hard in order to gain and maintain a certain level of social prominence and financial security. The Vanderhofs are zany, relaxed, and fun. Their philosophy is simple: since you can't take it with you, enjoy it while you can.

Our society lives that concept: Carpe diem, "seize the day," meaning take pleasure right now without concern for the future, because, after all, "you can't take it with you." Unfortunately, that philosophy is not entirely true. Although we can't take the stuff of life with us, we can send something on ahead. And being filled with the Spirit plays a crucial role in that process. Let me explain what I mean.

Choose Significance Over Self

We each choose one of two basic directions in life. Darrell Dement, the friend who followed me as pastor at my last church, said on his website, "If you can not find a purpose bigger than yourself, you become your own purpose."

Doesn't that ring true? Becoming our own purpose will never send anything ahead of us. Significance doesn't come from building a world around ourselves. Ironically, both the Vanderhofs and the Kirbys lived for the day, but each in a different way. But as we view life from God's perspective, we begin to value what lasts. We cherish making a lasting impact on others for the kingdom, or we treasure what God treasures.

We determine our treasure by what we value, where we place our priorities, and how we arrange our lives. Jesus suggested that we value heaven, and that our significance comes from what we have there rather than what we have on earth: "Do not store up for yourselves treasures on earth, where moth and rust destroy, and where thieves break in and steal. But store up for yourselves treasures in heaven, where moth and rust do not destroy, and where thieves do not break in and steal. For where your treasure is, there your heart will be also" (Matthew 6:19–21).

Jesus has promised us that we can send something ahead. We can build a spiritual retirement plan. The Vanderhofs were wrong after all; we can take something with us. But what Jesus didn't do was tell us *how* to do that, or what we should take. Specifically, what can we do now to build something significant enough to have an impact on our eternity in heaven?

Paul explained it in a parallel passage in 1 Timothy 6:17–19:

> Command those who are rich in this present world not to be arrogant nor to put their hope in wealth, which is so uncertain, but to put their hope in God, who richly provides us with everything for our enjoyment. Command them to do good, to be rich in good deeds, and to be generous and willing to share. In this way they will *lay up treasure for themselves as a firm foundation for the coming age,* so that they may take hold of the life that is truly life (emphasis added).

Let's break that passage down a bit. First, Paul reaffirms that we can't take worldly wealth with us to heaven. Admittedly, he didn't say exactly that, but it does represent what he meant. In the last sentence he echoed Jesus' concern about laying up treasure for heaven. But Paul adds, right in the middle, *how* we take something with us.

"Command them to do good, to be rich in good deeds, and to be generous and willing to share," or, make a spiritual impact on other people, do good to them, share with them generously. So, we take to heaven the spiritual impact we make on others. When we help bring people to Christ, we "take them" to heaven. When we help them grow spiritually, their growth "goes to heaven." And we build a spiritual legacy as we touch others for the kingdom.

We call that kind of activity "ministry." When we touch others, we avoid the trap of having ourselves as our purpose for life, and we build significance. Our lives matter for something beyond ourselves. We don't live just for ourselves, we touch others. And being filled with the Spirit provides the key to effective ministry, meaning that the Spirit builds significance into our lives.

Seek Significance

Let's explore just what ministry means.

MINISTRY'S EXPLANATION

We find the purpose of ministry given in Hebrews 1:14: "Are not all angels ministering spirits sent to *serve those who will inherit salvation?*" (emphasis added). The writer uses angels to give us an example of the purpose of ministry: to serve people spiritually. When we do good things to people, we serve them. Anything we do to help people know about God, or grow closer to him, is ministry—anything.

When we tell a neighbor who is struggling in his marriage that God can bring healing; that's ministry. When we set up the chairs before worship; that's ministry. When we replace the toilet paper in the church restrooms; that's ministry. When we "adopt" a child through World Vision; that's ministry. When we repaint the classroom walls at the church; that's ministry. When we teach a men's class or lead a women's group; that's ministry.

But let me qualify that: it is ministry when we do it out of our faith, to build the kingdom. Paul said in Romans 14:23, "Everything that does not come from faith is sin." You see, our motives play a crucial role. If we do anything begrudgingly or out of a sense of obligation or duty, we turn it from a ministry into a job. Jobs don't carry anything into heaven. We may even sin in doing a good thing, if we don't do it as a result of our faith. But a desire to serve can turn any job into a ministry. That ministry builds significance into our lives, and through it we build treasure in heaven.

Back in chapter 6 we learned that the Spirit gives each Christian a mix of spiritual gifts that make us unique individuals. Those gifts for ministry involve teaching, serving, leading, administering, showing mercy, and more. But ministry goes far beyond the list of gifts to include anything we do to bless people spiritually.

MINISTRY'S EXTENT

Ministry builds significance, and it extends to all believers. I grew up intimidated by the concept of being a "minister." After all, we paid the ministers, either as preachers, youth workers, or directors of Christian education. They went to Bible college. God called them to do what they did. They lived in continual contact with the Lord. They never even got tempted. (Well, maybe youth ministers did; ours even got mad a couple of times. Understandably, though, if you had known our group!)

But I knew that no one would pay me to be a minister. I hadn't gone to Bible college. I felt no call from God. And I certainly didn't live in continual touch with God. (I won't even mention the temptation issue here!)

Then, sometime in the early 1970s, I read Ray Stedman's book, *Body Life*. It shattered my misconceptions about the church and the Christian life. Stedman showed, too clearly for my comfort, that God designed all Christians to work as ministers. We would be paid, not necessarily with money, but with the significance of touching lives. We needed Christian education, but not necessarily in a formal Bible college. Churches could provide that education. God did call all of us to minister, even if not professionally. And yes, we all should continually walk with God—and resist temptation.

I was right about the distinctives of ministry; I had just applied them too narrowly. Each dimension applied to each Christian. What passage did Stedman use? Ephesians 4:11–15:

> It was he who gave some to be apostles, some to
> be prophets, some to be evangelists, and some
> to be pastors and teachers, *to prepare God's
> people for works of service,* so that the body of
> Christ may be built up until we all reach unity in
> the faith and in the knowledge of the Son of

God and become mature, attaining to the whole measure of the fullness of Christ.

Then we will no longer be infants, tossed back and forth by the waves, and blown here and there by every wind of teaching and by the cunning and craftiness of men in their deceitful scheming. Instead, speaking the truth in love, we will in all things grow up into him who is the Head, that is, Christ (emphasis added).

We all reach the goal of maturity as the leaders of the church (yes, the preachers, youth workers, education directors, and those we pay to give great amounts of their time) train us to minister. The key word word here is *service*. Again, we see ministry as action taken to benefit others spiritually. Such ministry helps us all grow spiritually, and it has an eternal impact on heaven.

Back in Civil War days, wealthy people could hire others to take their place in the army. They escaped the hardships, wounds, and death that threatened the soldiers. But as far as my research shows, none of these people who hired others to take their place ever became a hero. None ever received a medal for valor. None ever reached significance.

Many Christians today hire others to do their ministry. They believe if they give enough money, they can escape the task. In so doing, they choose to avoid significance. They miss God's design that all of us should minister. Remember, ministry provides the key to significance above self. Let me share two reasons that ministry leads to significance.

The Ministry Benefits

When we invest ourselves in serving others, we see the impact multiplied. If just a few members in a church engage in ministry, the overall impact is minimized. But when all get involved, amazing results occur.

One of my favorite studies explored why people came to church the first time. Having been in the pastoral ministry and seen the importance of pastors to the kingdom, I expected that aspect to rank near the top. But out of eight factors, it ranked sixth, with less than 1 percent of first-time visitors coming because of the direct or indirect influence of the pastor. That's humbling!

But 15 percent came because a relative invited them, and 48 percent because a friend did so, or 63 percent of first-time visitors came because a non-pastor invited them. That kind of ministry makes a significant impact for the kingdom of God. Another study indicated that up to 75 percent of unchurched people would be very open to attending a church if a trusted friend or relative asked them.

So, when we minister, we have great potential to expand the kingdom of God. Doesn't that give us a sense of genuine significance? But ministry does more.

The Ministers' Benefit

Ministry benefits the ministers in two ways. First, like a muscle, the Christian life grows stronger with exercise. Not only do we need good nutrition, we need activity. That activity changes us for the good. Let's look at Ephesians 4:13–14 to see what the apostle Paul says will occur when we use our abilities for ministry:

> … until we all reach *unity in the faith* and in the *knowledge of the Son of God* and *become mature,* attaining to the whole measure of the fullness of Christ.

> Then we will *no longer be infants, tossed back and forth* by the waves, and blown here and there by every wind of teaching and by the cunning and craftiness of men in their deceitful scheming (emphasis added).

Ministry causes the ministers to reach unity, to know God better, to mature, to become stable, and to be able to resist the tides of popular culture. That sounds like a significant result, one that only comes through ministry.

Second, we ministers benefit by gaining rewards in heaven. In 1 Corinthians 3:10-15, Paul talks about how the Day of Judgment relates to what we do with our earthly lives. His basic premise: how we use our resources for our few years on earth determines what we get out of eternity in heaven:

> By the grace God has given me, I laid a foundation as an expert builder, and someone else is building on it. But each one should be careful how he builds. For no one can lay any foundation other than the one already laid, which is Jesus Christ. If any man builds on this foundation using gold, silver, costly stones, wood, hay or straw, his work will be shown for what it is, because the Day will bring it to light. It will be revealed with fire, and the fire will test the quality of each man's work. If what he has built survives, he will receive his reward. If it is burned up, he will suffer loss; he himself will be saved, but only as one escaping through the flames.

Let's hit the highlights. First, we must build our lives on the foundation of a relationship with Jesus. Second, *how* we build on that foundation impacts heaven. On the Day of Judgment, if we have ministered well, we will receive some kind of reward. But if we have ministered poorly, we will enter into heaven with smoke on our coattails and very little else. I *suspect* that our entrance into heaven will influence our entire stay in heaven. That is, I don't think God will give us an extra shiny crown that goes back to normal after a few billion years.

Whether we minister well or poorly, we will still get into heaven, since we are connected to Jesus. But some of us will receive something extra. Based on what? Based on how we affected others, on how much we sacrificed to build treasures for heaven. Yes, ministry will result in sacrifices: of our time, our resources, our energy, and our talents. But rather than being an expense, we should look on these as investments that will last for eternity. That sounds like a much better rate of return than we will ever get on the stock market.

So far, we have talked about how ministry builds significance into our lives. But we haven't mentioned how being filled with the Spirit fits into that equation. Let's look at that connection.

Spirit-Empowered Significance

Just as it did in high school, the idea of ministry intimidates me. It requires sacrifice, as we have just mentioned. Most of us prefer to avoid that kind of commitment; we had rather experience comfort, ease, and security. And the stakes are high: if we don't minister well, people can suffer—perhaps eternally—as a result of our negligence or ineptness. I would rather avoid doing things with such a high cost of failure. I don't want to be responsible for not sharing God's truth accurately if that failure might result in some other person's rejecting God.

So, many Christians resist ministry involvement. Typically, 10 percent of church members do 90 percent of the work. In my last church, we identified 60 percent of regular adult attendees who had some type of known ministry. That is an *awesome* percentage, but even so, nearly one half of the adults had no identifiable ministry. That is an *awful* percentage.

When God guides us to a ministry, he also provides all we need to do it well. When the task seems overwhelming, the resources provided by God exceed the need. (Well, let's be totally honest—they at least meet the need.) And the Spirit-filled life opens up the resources.

I wish I knew who wrote this little poem so I could acknowledge the source of the wisdom in it that has helped me many times over the years:

> When God is going to do something wonderful,
> He begins with a difficulty.
> If it's going to be something very wonderful,
> He begins with an impossibility.

Here is an example. After seventeen years of ministry, he thought himself a failure and was ready to quit. He began at a church with twenty-five people, and after trying every program to make it grow, two years later he had seventeen people, and five of those were his family. Then he started a Bible study, learned to rely on the Spirit, and things began to change. His name: Chuck Smith. The Bible study: it became Calvary Chapel. Calvary Chapel played a central role in the Jesus Movement, has grown to bout 15,000 attenders, and has spun off hundreds of other churches.

Will it always happen that way? Probably not. But it can, if we stay faithful to the ministry given us by God, and if we rely on the Spirit.

But when God leads us, we can attempt the impossible, which often results in "something very wonderful." I began my last ministry in a church that had just passed its seventy-second birthday. The average life of a church is eighty years, and this one had been in decline for many years. Not long before I came, they did a study that suggested the church would last five years, maybe ten at the maximum, if they continued as they were. Some wanted to hire a semi-retired pastor, play out the string, and let the church die slowly. Revival seemed impossible.

But they decided to attempt it. The church made a number of changes to the facility, they added a new contemporary worship service, they launched a marketing campaign, and invested a lot of money, and in two years attendance had doubled. Since then, a new pastor has come in, and new faces continue to be seen. Something that seemed impossible became possible. Why? They trusted in God to do impossible ministry.

When we allow the Spirit to fill us, he provides us with all the resources we need for effective ministry, to build significance into our lives. I have become convinced, through studying Scripture and living the Christian life, that we can minister effectively *only* when the Spirit fills us. But, in practice, how does this principle work? How does the Spirit make an impact on our ministry?

Spirit-Given Gifts—Tools for Ministry

I don't want to retrace chapter 6, but we do need to review it here. Before the Spirit guides us into a ministry, he gives us the tools to do it. We call these tools "spiritual gifts." Let's review four basic principles of the gifts of the Spirit.

First, each Christian receives a spiritual gift: *"As each one has received a gift,* minister it to one another, as good stewards of the manifold grace of God"(1 Peter 4:10 NKJV, emphasis added). I am fascinated that the Greek word translated "gift" in this verse is *charisma,* from which we get *charismatic.* Since each Christian receives a *charisma,* then according to the Bible, all Christians are charismatic, even if they never speak in tongues. I realize that concept doesn't match the popular definition of charismatic, but it seems that it does to God. That's good enough for me.

Second, we receive that gift so we can best minister to others, according to the second phrase in our verse, "minister it to one another." We don't receive gifts primarily to feel good about ourselves, or even to get closer to God. Gifts are given to be used to minister to others.

Third, the Spirit gives these gifts as he desires. Yes, we can ask for a specific gift, but the Spirit controls who gets what, according to 1 Corinthians 12:11: "All these [various gifts] are the work of one and the same Spirit, and he gives them to each one, just as he determines."

Why? If the Spirit fills and leads us, then he needs to be sure we have what we need to do what he assigns us. I may want the gift of music, but the Spirit placed me in a teaching role. To follow where the Spirit leads me, do I need what I want, or what the Spirit wants? When we think of it in those terms, the answer is obvious.

Fourth, each Christian has a unique gift or skill set, as we saw in chapter 6. In 1 Corinthians 12:12 the apostle Paul summarizes how we are all different: "The body is a unit, though it is made up of many parts; and though all its parts are many, they form one body. So it is with Christ." Doesn't that add to our significance, that no one else is exactly like we are? We have significance because we have uniqueness.

Now, let's go back to our main point. We develop significance from making an impact on others spiritually. Spiritual gifts enable us to make that impact. And who directs the gifting process? The Spirit. Again, the more we yield to the Spirit, the more he can do in us and through us. So as we allow the Spirit to fill us, his gifts to us reach their maximum ministry potential and effect. But the Spirit does even more to build significant ministry in our lives.

SPIRITUAL TRANSFORMATION—CHARACTER FOR MINISTRY

The preceding section dealt with the tools of ministry. This section touches on the character of the minister.

One of the important ministries available to us is prayer, and our character plays a central role in how effective we are in our prayer life, as we see in James 5:16: "Therefore confess your sins to each other and pray for each other so that you may be healed. *The prayer of a righteous man is powerful and effective*" (emphasis added).

We can easily draw a reverse implication that the prayers of a person who isn't righteous are not very powerful or effective. The conclusion: our character has an impact upon our ministry effectiveness. Again, the Spirit plays a vital role in crafting a new character for us.

In a previous book I explored how the fruit of the Spirit allows us to develop God's character, with Galatians 5:22–23 as the primary text. But even more, 2 Corinthians 3:18 reveals the role of the Spirit in changing our character: "And we, who with unveiled faces all reflect the Lord's glory, are being transformed into his likeness with ever-increasing glory, which comes from the Lord, who is the Spirit."

The Spirit transforms us into the likeness of the Lord. That phenomenal change of character provides the foundation for greater ministry effectiveness, which leads to greater significance. But that's not all.

SPIRIT-LED MINISTRY—THE GLORY OF MINISTRY

The Bible describes ministry as glorious, although at times I am tempted to disagree. When a Sunday school teacher has to deal with five year olds who bite each other, it doesn't *feel* glorious. And on a church workday, pulling overgrown weeds until blisters pop up on sore hands doesn't *feel* glorious. Let's look carefully at Paul's description of ministry in 2 Corinthians 3:6-8:

> He [the Lord] has made us *competent as ministers* of a new covenant—not of the letter but of the Spirit; for the letter kills, but the Spirit gives life.
>
> Now if the ministry that brought death, which was engraved in letters on stone, came with glory, so that the Israelites could not look steadily at the face of Moses because of its glory, fading though it was, will not *the ministry of the Spirit be even more glorious?* (emphasis added).

We have already seen how God makes us competent to minister. But in his Word he also describes the ministry of the Spirit as glorious. When we minister in the Spirit, while being continually filled, we experience glory.

One of those little five-year-olds (not a biter!) would come into our prayer time before Sunday school, pray a simple prayer, and we saw the glory. When a visitor saw the carefully kept property and said, "These people care about God," we experienced glory.

How do we minister in the Spirit? We use our gifts. We let the Spirit transform our character. We yearn to make an impact on people for God. We minister as an outflow of our faith. Whenever we do these things, we see glory in that ministry.

SPIRITUAL PRIVILEGES—A MINISTRY OF HOPE

Ministry at any level can become discouraging. We work hard, but we get little appreciation—and a lot of grief. We sometimes see far fewer results than we anticipated. But we can change our perspective on ministry, and see it transformed.

Soon after the reference to *"the ministry of the Spirit,"* Paul wrote, "Therefore, since through God's mercy we have this ministry, we do not lose heart" (2 Corinthians 4:1).

Do you think of ministry as a privilege? As something God gives us *in mercy?* Sometimes I feel that ministry is punishment for something terrible I did in a past life. But when I think that way, I am wrong. God *graces* us with the privilege of serving others, of taking them to heaven. We tend to think we do God a favor when we accept a ministry; in truth, God does us a favor when he offers us one.

So, we should value the privilege God gives us to make a spiritual impact upon others. That attitude helps us not to lose heart when things get difficult and frustrating. We easily get discouraged when we think of ministry as ineffective or unimportant. But what an honor we have to participate in the process by which the Spirit transforms other believers into the likeness of the Lord, from one stage of glory to another. How glorious it is to be trusted with a small piece of the work of the Spirit in which we are allowed to share. That is significant.

SPIRIT-FILLED MINISTRY—A MINISTRY OF IMPORTANCE

We can determine the importance of a task by the tools assigned to complete it. For example, if we are given a shotgun, we are not given the task of hunting ants. In ministry, God gives us the spiritual equivalent of a shotgun.

The early church grew explosively, and the apostles kept a close eye on all aspects of the ministry—until it became too difficult, so they began to give it away. One ministry they gave away seemed to be a simple one—distributing food evenly to the widows in the church.

We would think that the early disciples of Christ would have been able to handle that simple task. But we would be wrong. Let's examine the job requirements, from Acts 6:2-3:

> So the Twelve gathered all the disciples together
> and said, "It would not be right for us to neglect
> the ministry of the word of God in order to wait
> on tables. Brothers, choose seven men from

among you who are known to be *full of the Spirit* and wisdom. We will turn this responsibility over to them" (emphasis added).

It was a simple job of waiting tables, a ministry anyone should be able to do. What was the first requirement? That these new ministers be *filled with the Spirit.* Why the shotgun for something so simple? Maybe because ministry is never so simple.

Think with me. Ministry means making a spiritual impact on others. When we make that impact on others, we build treasure in heaven. That makes ministry pretty important, doesn't it?

All ministry combats the forces of Satan. *All* ministry strives to advance the kingdom of God. *All* ministry is significant. *All* ministry needs to be Spirit filled.

As we allow the Spirit to fill us, we become competent to carry out ministry. As we minister, we build significance. As we build significance, we lay up treasure in heaven. That is not a bad deal!

Chapter 9

Supernatural Power to Transcend Differences

We human beings possess a disturbing tendency to allow our differences to divide us. We mistrust those who differ from us, we suspect their motives, and we build a protective wall of distance between them and us. After the recent war in Iraq, mass graves were found representing the final resting place of perhaps 300,000 Iraqis killed by fellow Iraqis of different political or religious persuasions. Even now, Iraqi Shiite and Sunni Muslims struggle for supremacy. In the Holy Land, Israelis and Palestinians bomb and fire rockets at one another, yet both trace their descent to Abraham. In Liberia, President Charles Taylor stirred up revolution in his nation and neighboring countries where as many as tens of thousands of people were killed, raped, kidnapped, or maimed.

But we in the church do little better when it comes to unity. In one town in which I served as pastor, two different churches split over the color of carpeting in the fellowship hall! One source says that Christian faith groups can be divided into four meta-groups: Roman Catholic, Orthodox, Protestant, and Anglican. Christian groups can also fit into different "wings": conservative, mainline, or liberal. Theological belief systems divide us; Calvinism versus Arminianism provides just one example. There are at least fifteen religious "families," such as the Baptist family, the Lutheran family, and so on.

And of course we have our denominations, from the Amish to followers of the Way. In America about a thousand denominations give themselves the name of Christian. I have found thirty-eight different flavors of Catholic, and even the Mormons have nearly a hundred different splinter groups. The unity movement in which I grew up split into three major wings, and who knows how many smaller segments, which seems to be a strange pattern for unity.

Remember the plaintive quote by Rodney King, whose beating set off riots in Los Angeles a few years ago? "Why can't we all just get along?" That is a very good question. But our concern isn't so much why the *world* can't get along, but why can't *Christians* get along? Let me suggest that we can't get along because we don't choose to let the Spirit fill us. Only when we do the latter can we do the former. Only being filled allows us to transcend our differences and get along with one another.

Let's explore this whole issue of unity, differences, and being filled with the Spirit.

Cherish Unity

Unity fills the pages of the New Testament, and we need to adjust our attitudes toward it so they match God's.

GOD'S POINT OF VIEW—COME TOGETHER

Let's begin by exploring just some of the passages in which God reveals his will for his people, as expressed in the words of the apostle Paul. Spend some time reading these passages; try to get into God's mind as you ponder them.

> I appeal to you, brothers, in the name of our Lord Jesus Christ, that all of you *agree* with one another so that there may be *no divisions* among you and that you may be *perfectly united* in mind and thought (1 Corinthians 1:10, emphasis added).

The body is a unit, though it is made up of many parts; and though all its parts are many, they form *one body.* So it is with Christ. For we were all baptized by one Spirit into *one body*— whether Jews or Greeks, slave or free—and we were all *given the one Spirit* to drink (1 Corinthians 12:12–13, emphasis added).

Finally, brothers, good-by. *Aim for perfection,* listen to my appeal, be *of one mind, live in peace.* And the God of love and peace will be with you (2 Corinthians 13:11, emphasis added).

From the first passage, we see that we need to be united in mind and thought. We can disagree on non-essential issues, but we need to be agreeable. In the second passage, we see how the Spirit puts us together. Again, we will return to this point, but keep in mind the link between the Spirit and our unity. The third passage gives us a goal of aiming for perfection (please notice that it is aiming, not hitting!). We aim for perfection when we value being of one mind and living in peace.

Why does God value unity despite differences? I think it flows from his identity.

GOD'S NATURE—THREE PERSONS UNITED AS ONE

In Jesus' last night before his death, he revealed his viewpoint about unity and the Trinity. In John 17:20–23 Jesus prayed for us, those who would believe through the centuries as a result of the work of the original disciples. In so doing, he focused on the unity between the Father and Son:

"My prayer is not for them alone. I pray also for those who will believe in me through their message, *that all of them may be one,* Father, *just as you are in me and I am in you.* May they also be in us so that the world may believe that you have sent me. I have given them the glory that you gave me, that *they may be one as we are one:* I in them and you in me. May they be brought to *complete unity* to let the world know that you sent me and have loved them even as you have loved me" (John 17:20–23, emphasis added).

Let's take a quick glance at 2 Corinthians 3:17–18 to see that Jesus and the Spirit are likewise separate individuals united as one:

Now the *Lord is the Spirit,* and where the Spirit of the Lord is, there is freedom. And we, who with unveiled faces all reflect the *Lord's glory,* are being transformed into his likeness with ever-increasing glory, which comes from *the Lord, who is the Spirit* (emphasis added).

Let's put some concepts together. First, the word *Trinity* expresses the concept that in one God we find three Persons so united that they can be called one—God the Father, God the Son, and God the Holy Spirit. These verses make that point fairly clear.

Second, God wants followers of Jesus to be as united as he and Jesus. He wants us to be so completely connected that we could be called "one"—just like God. That may scare us, but we can't escape it. Christians are to become more Christlike, as we saw in the last passage. And Christlikeness means unity. When we choose the Christian life, we choose to become like the Father and Son in character.

Third, glory is mentioned again. Jesus linked glory and unity in John 17:22: "I have given them the glory that you gave me, that they may be one as we are one." The Corinthians passage, in expressing the unity of Jesus and the Spirit, proclaims that we share in God's glory. How? By our unity with one another, and with him.

How does all this work? I suspect that as we become more Christlike, more united in both directions, people can see more of God in us. And that looks good! Jesus even said that our unity would be a prime factor in causing people to believe in him.

Understand Unity

You may ask the same questions I do: "It sounds good, but let's get practical. Are denominations wrong? If I give myself to unity, then specifically how do I have to change? What does this unity look like?"

I don't want to get too specific, because I think the Spirit will express unity differently in different places. In one town, two churches from different denominations merged into one new church to increase their effectiveness. But the Spirit may not call all churches to do the same. In another place, dozens of churches hired a coordinator to lead their unity efforts and shared ministries. But the Spirit may not call all churches to do the same.

Let's be sensitive to the leading of the Spirit in this area of learning what unity looks like, but let me share four foundational principles of unity that might help us.

UNIVERSAL

The Spirit lives within each follower of Jesus and wants to fill each believer. His goal of unity among believers extends to each of us. Let's return to our passage in John 17:20-21: "My prayer is not for them alone. I pray also for those who will believe in me through their message, that *all of them may be one*" (emphasis added).

Jesus prayed for us, his followers of all ages since the original believers. What was his prayer? That all of us may be one: not just that the Baptists would unite, nor just Presbyterians, not just the members of a local congregation who have been battling, not just the various churches in a city, but *all of us*.

Jesus kind of eliminated our "wiggle room." He made it clear that he wants *all* of his followers to be united: period. So, the following principles apply to each of us and all of us.

OBSERVABLE

This aspect of unity may present our most difficult challenge. An elder at my former church and I were talking about unity, and he suggested that all Christians already possess all the unity God desires, since we are united in the body of his Son. I told him I thought that was a "cop-out," because "it lets us off the hook too easily" (no, I didn't put it in those words, I was much more gracious).

Why did I disagree with the idea that we Christians already have all the unity God desires? Because it just doesn't represent reality. Otherwise, why did Jesus have to pray for something we already have? That makes no sense. Jesus prayed that something in the future might happen; he didn't thank the Father that something had already occurred in the past. Jesus looked forward to something different.

What was that "something different" for which Jesus looked and prayed? An observable unity between believers that unbelievers could see and to which they would be drawn. As evidence, go to verse 23: "May they be *brought to complete unity* to let the world know that you sent me and have loved them even as you have loved me" (emphasis added).

First, we have an instant spiritual unity. But we must be *brought to complete unity.* That complete unity is a process in which we grow as we allow the Spirit to fill, lead, and empower us. Complete unity requires an ongoing cooperation with the Spirit.

Second, unbelievers can see this unity and be drawn by it and to it. As they see us overcome innate differences that tend to divide us, as they see us overcome our self-will, they realize that something supernatural is taking place—something beyond normal human experience. I think this unity will look different in different times and places, but it will be seen by those outside the church.

Sacrificial

We have already seen that Jesus wants complete unity, not partial, and that our unity should match the unity between him and the Father. When I think of that kind of unity, the first concept that pops into my mind is sacrifice. The Father sacrificed the Son. The Son sacrificed the comfort of heaven, and his holiness, to carry out the will of the Father.

Yes, we tend to sacrifice for our local churches. We give of our money, our time, our energy, and our resources. We do the same for other believers who share our same viewpoints and values. But do we limit our sacrifice? Does how we sacrifice for believers outside our church and circle of friends demonstrate complete unity?

Here is just one example. Some of us pastors from San Pedro, California, sensed God leading us to hold a joint worship service to which we would invite all the churches in town to worship Christ together, as a united body. We talked about the best time, and difficulties arose. All had worship services on Sunday morning, so that time slot was eliminated. Some had Sunday night worship, so that slot went off the board. A few had Saturday evening worship, so another option disappeared. On Friday nights the local high school had football games, and we wanted to meet in the stadium.

Not many options remained, and then one pastor said, "If we want to demonstrate unity, and if the Father and Son sacrificed for one another, what if we all made a big sacrifice, and sacrificed Sunday morning? Let's not meet as individual congregations that week, let's just worship together as the church of San Pedro."

Eventually, twenty-five churches closed their doors on Sunday morning in September for San Pedro Celebrates Christ: a small sample of sacrificial unity.

FUNCTIONAL

Again, exactly how we go about establishing unity will vary, but when I think of the purpose of unity, I realize how far short of God's will and desire we fall. Let's survey John 17 again. In verse 4, Jesus acknowledged to the Father that his work on earth was almost done: "I have brought you glory on earth by completing *the work you gave me to do*" (emphasis added).

Then, he passed on to the disciples the continuation of that same purpose of reconciling God and people: "As you sent me into the world, *I have sent them into the world*" (v. 18, emphasis added).

We often call this the Great Commission; Jesus gave us the task of reaching the world with the message of forgiveness and faith in Christ. Now, notice the next step. He clarified the task and provided a means to accomplish it: "May they be brought to complete unity *to let the world know* that you sent me and have loved them even as you have loved me"(v. 23, emphasis added).

A Spirit-led unity will focus on working together to reach the world for Christ. We already do some of that working together for a common cause. Billy Graham crusades bring together hundreds of churches that rarely cooperate, and that's good. World Vision and other parachurch ministries reach across denominational lines, and that's good. Churches in a community often work together to meet the social needs of people, to feed the hungry and care for the homeless, and that's good.

But can we honestly say that our current level of cooperation represents complete unity? Can we honestly say that we cooperate strategically to reach our world for Christ? Maybe we need to rethink what it means to be filled with the Spirit.

Unity seems pretty important to God, doesn't it? But it doesn't always happen.

Despise Divisions

We have seen God's desire for unity, but understanding unity requires having a coin with two sides.

When young, many of us cheated by having a coin with two "heads" and no "tails." So when we called "heads," we could feel confident about winning. Those of us with regular coins sometimes tried to scam our friends with the line, "Heads I win, tails you lose," but that didn't work very often.

We have God's point of view when we both cherish unity and avoid divisions. I am amazed at the number of passages that deal with believers overcoming differences.

GOD'S POINT OF VIEW—AVOID DIVISIONS

A study I once did on church discipline surprised me quite a bit. I expected the majority of discipline to deal with sexual immorality, since Christians today tend to make that the big sin.

But I found more passages encouraging the church to discipline those who divide the church and have a contentious spirit. Without minimizing the damage of sexual sin, could it be that division might bring even more destruction?

May I suggest that we carefully read these following passages; they represent the disfavor with which God views disunity. May we adjust our attitudes to come more in line with God's.

> I urge you, brothers, to watch out for those who *cause divisions* and *put obstacles* in your way that are contrary to the teaching you have learned. *Keep away from them.* For such people are not serving our Lord Christ, but their own appetites. By smooth talk and flattery they deceive the minds of naive people (Romans 16:17-18, emphasis added).

> I appeal to you, brothers, in the name of our Lord Jesus Christ, that all of you *agree with one another* so that there may be *no divisions* among you and that you may be *perfectly united* in mind and thought. My brothers, some from Chloe's household have informed me that there are *quarrels* among you. What I mean is this: One of you says, "I follow Paul"; another, "I follow Apollos"; another, "I follow Cephas"; still another, "I follow Christ."

> *Is Christ divided?* Was Paul crucified for you? Were you baptized into the name of Paul? (1 Corinthians 1:10-13, emphasis added).

> In the following directives I have no praise for you, for your meetings do more harm than good. In the first place, I hear that when you come together as a church, there are *divisions* among you, and to some extent I believe it. No doubt there have to be *differences* among you to

show which of you have God's approval (1 Corinthians 11:17–19, emphasis added, and notice that this last sentence seems full of sarcasm, not praise).

The acts of the *sinful nature* are obvious: sexual immorality, impurity and debauchery; idolatry and witchcraft; *hatred, discord, jealousy, fits of rage, selfish ambition, dissensions, factions and envy;* drunkenness, orgies, and the like. I warn you, as I did before, that those who live like this will *not inherit* the kingdom of God (Galatians 5:19–21, emphasis added, and notice that seven of the fifteen acts directly deal with disunity).

But avoid *foolish controversies* and genealogies and *arguments and quarrels* about the law, because these are unprofitable and useless. Warn a *divisive person* once, and then warn him a second time. After that, *have nothing to do with him.* You may be sure that such a man is warped and sinful; he is self-condemned (Titus 3:9–11, emphasis added).

We need to view divisiveness as a major sin. We don't always do so. We can easily rationalize that everyone is entitled to their own opinion and that we should not try to create mindless robots in the church. Both of these statements are true. But when we use them to avoid seeing the tremendous importance of contentiousness, then we apply them wrongly.

Why does God seem to despise divisiveness so much? First, it contradicts the unity of his nature, which we just explored. Second, it makes evangelism ineffective, which we mentioned in the John 17 passage. People just aren't attracted to people who fight. Third, it makes life painful for God's people. We find joy difficult to maintain when we struggle with others. Remember, "God has called us to live in peace" (1 Corinthians 7:15).

If the lack of unity holds so much significance, then what causes us not to get along with other Christians? Let's identify some basic causes.

Valid Differences

For too long, Christians have looked down on those who believe or behave differently: "They're charismatic, and you just can't trust people who let their emotions drive them." "Anyone who doesn't speak in tongues lives such a boring, powerless Christian life." "I call contemporary worship '7-11 services': you sing seven words eleven times." "Traditional church services feel like a funeral." "If we worship with people outside our denomination, then we dilute our witness to the truth."

I have heard these and similar words repeatedly; you probably have also. We tend to judge those with differences with a bit of harshness; we prefer our group, doing things our way, not having our beliefs questioned, and we rejoice that we are not like "them" (see Luke 18:11).

Although we don't usually divide over central theological concepts such as the Trinity, faith, or the Person of God, our differences are still real and valid. They have an impact on the way we minister, the church we attend, and the people with whom we associate. But differences shouldn't grow into divisiveness, in which we separate from each other and judge one another.

The apostle Peter and a soldier named Cornelius demonstrated that truth, even though they had some valid differences, as told in Acts 10. Those differences changed how the early church ministered. But they dealt with them and overcame them.

I am amazed at how these two men differed. Cornelius served as a soldier, Peter worked as a fisherman. As an officer, Cornelius commanded others. As a self-employed laborer, Peter probably had little if any authority over others.. Cornelius had a Roman background, with all the pride that came with being part of the world's leading empire. Peter had a Jewish background, with all the pride that came with being part of the Chosen People. Cornelius likely had a slave background, while Peter was fiercely independent. Although a devout man who often prayed, Cornelius probably wouldn't qualify as a Jew, but Peter had been born and raised one. Cornelius had traveled the world; he was a real cosmopolitan. Peter had always been in or near Israel and led a blossoming church pretty much limited then to Jews.

If events followed their natural course, their lives would probably never have intersected. And if their paths had crossed by chance, each likely would have ignored the other as beneath his notice. But Peter had access to something Cornelius needed, and God wanted Cornelius to mark a milestone in the growth of the new church.

So one day as Cornelius prayed, he had a vision in which God told him to call for this stranger, a man named Peter. Soon after, at about noon, Peter went to the roof to pray where he, too, had a vision. Probably because of his growling stomach, Peter saw a sheet with all sorts of animals, including the unclean ones that Jews couldn't eat. God said to him, "Kill and eat."

When Peter complained that he had never eaten any of these unclean animals, God told him not to call unclean what God had made clean. Peter didn't yet realize it, but God primarily was talking about people. The previously unclean non-Jews could now become spiritually clean through faith in Jesus. So when the messengers from Cornelius appeared and announced that God had instructed Cornelius to call for Peter, he overcame the differences and went along with them.

Look at his conclusion as expressed to Cornelius and the entourage who had gathered at his home to hear what Peter had to say: "You are well aware that it is against our law for a Jew to associate with a Gentile or visit him. But God has shown me that I should not call any man impure or unclean. ... I now realize how true it is that *God does not show favoritism* but accepts men from every nation who fear him and do what is right" (Acts 10:28, 34–35, emphasis added).

Peter and Cornelius had valid differences, but overcame them in their obedience to God. Peter shared the good news of Jesus, Cornelius accepted Christ and was baptized, and the church of Jewish Christians began reaching out to non-Jews. Did that change make a difference? Paul and his companions continued that outreach to non-Jews; listen to how others described them just nine years later: "These people who have been turning the world upside down have come here also" (see Acts 17:6 NRSV).

Believers today also have significant differences, the type that often cause us to divide. They definitely prevent "business as usual." But here, Peter and Cornelius overcame their differences and changed their world. So, even though valid differences can bring division, they can be overcome.

Self Will

Often our division does not come so much from differences as from selfishness. We want our way, others get in our way, and we battle. James, the brother of Jesus, recognized this situation:

> What causes fights and quarrels among you? Don't they come from your desires that battle within you? You want something but don't get it. You kill and covet, but you cannot have what you want. You quarrel and fight. You do not have, because you do not ask God. When you ask, you do not receive, because you ask with wrong motives, that you may spend what you get on your pleasures (James 4:1–3).

With the experience of decades in pastoral ministry, I am convinced that money troubles don't lie at the heart of most marriage problems. The issue is who *controls* the money.

That issue of control spills over into every relationship: we can't live in peace if we struggle for supremacy.

When we allow either our differences or our self-will to inhibit unity, then we quench the Spirit. We keep the Spirit from doing the work he desires to do in us. So, we need to cooperate with him.

Enhance Unity

My aunt Shirley had a dog and cat who each loved her as deeply as they hated one other. At night, the cat would cuddle by Shirley's head at the pillow, while the dog nestled at her feet. One night she awoke to a huge ruckus. While sleeping, the dog and cat had accidentally touched one another, realized it, and began to fight. Only her presence calmed them down, and only after their beloved owner had received some scratches.

Those three provide a marvelous analogy for our unity through the Spirit. Despite our valid differences, despite our tendencies to strive for our self-will, when we give the Spirit full reign in our lives, then our shared love for him can overcome any obstacles to our unity. Let's examine how we can enhance unity through being filled.

It's Already Here!

Back in my single days, I met Shandra, and sparks of interest flew in both directions. But even though we mutually pursued the relationship, we just couldn't make it work. Different personalities combined with different expectations of the relationship, and we lived in different towns. Even though we both wanted to connect, we couldn't.

Have you ever had a relationship like that? It may have been with a person of the opposite sex, a friend, a family member, or a church. Somehow, despite your best efforts, it just never seemed to work out. That kind of thing happens to all of us. Sometimes it seems that "we just can't get there from here."

Perhaps the best news about unity is that we don't have to work to develop it, we don't have to wonder if we can "make it happen." Rather, the Spirit just gives it. We are never told to create unity, just to keep it going.

"Make every effort to *keep* the unity of the Spirit through the bond of peace" (Ephesians 4:3, emphasis added). Other translations offer some different slants on that word *keep*. The *New American Standard Version* has *preserve*, the *New Revised Standard Version* uses *maintain*. But each recognizes that unity already exists; we don't create or build it. We just maintain it, we preserve it, and we keep it. We don't allow it to decrease. We work to increase it on a practical level.

Have you ever seen an abandoned house? It seems to decay much quicker when left empty than it would if people lived in it. Unity works the same way. The more we use it, the stronger it gets. The less we use it, the weaker it gets. But it's a gift—a gift from the Spirit, which leads us to the main point of this entire chapter.

IT'S SPIRIT BASED

Let's go back to Ephesians 4:3: "Make every effort to keep *the unity of the Spirit* through the bond of peace" (emphasis added).

What's the source of our unity? The Spirit.

You may want to review the section titled **Cherish Unity** and read the passages there. And, focus on 1 Corinthians 12:13: "For we were all baptized *by one Spirit into one body*—whether Jews or Greeks, slave or free—and we were all *given the one Spirit to drink*" (emphasis added).

The Spirit baptizes us into the one church, the body of Christ. We all drink from the same Spirit. So, all followers of Jesus have received the Spirit (see Acts 2:38), we are united, and we need to preserve that which the Spirit gives us. We can't escape these facts.

Now, what is the secret to maintaining this unity? Think with me as we survey this section of Ephesians. Chapter 4 focuses on the proper functioning of the church, which begins with a dynamic, Spirit-based unity. Chapter 5 focuses on living like God: "Be imitators of God, therefore, as dearly loved children" (Ephesians 5:1).

In this context, how do we build this Spirit-based unity and imitate God? Let's go back to the normal Christian life just a few verses later in 5:18: "Do not get drunk on wine, which leads to debauchery. Instead, *be filled with the Spirit*" (emphasis added).

The Spirit unites us, and he wants us to grow ever deeper into that unity. He fills us so we can do so. When we disagree, divide, and cause dissension by breaking into groups, we quench the Spirit. We hinder his work in us. We can't be filled with him.

This concept has caused me to re-evaluate my entire Christian life. Not only is it normal to be filled, it is normal to be united. And we hinder the work of God, through his Spirit, when we resist that unity.

We have seen what it means to be united. Think with me. Can we honestly say that most Christians, across denominational lines, across church families, have an observable unity? Would most Christians identify themselves as Spirit-filled?

All too often, we miss the mark. And to miss the mark is to sin. The Spirit yearns to unite us. And we resist. The Spirit yearns to fill us, so that we may have available all the power God desires. And we resist.

So, as we have seen, the first step is to let the Spirit do whatever he wants to do in us. We must allow the Spirit to fill us. Until we do that, we *cannot* be united as God desires. Once we do that, then we can take the second step.

IT REQUIRES SUBMISSION TO OTHERS

We can submit to the Spirit—not easily perhaps, but we can do it—since we know that he is God, all wise and all loving. But when we return to our primary Ephesians 5 passage about being filled with the Spirit, it becomes more difficult. Verses 5:18 through 6:9 all flow from the command in verse 18 to be filled with the Spirit. We examined this passage back in chapter 2, and it fits into the following outline:

Be filled with the Spirit (5:18).
1. Speaking to one another spiritually (5:19).
2. Singing and making music to the Lord (5:19).
3. Giving thanks always (5:20).
4. *Submitting to one another* (5:21, emphasis added).
   a. How husbands and wives submit (5:22-33).
   b. How children and parents submit (6:1-4).
   c. How employees and employers submit (6:5-9).

The greatest part of this section, twenty-two of twenty-five verses, teaches us how to yield to one another in our relationships. Now, won't submitting to others deal with the two major obstacles to unity that we have discussed?

We often divide because of *differences* between us, but didn't Peter and Cornelius submit to one another, to the needs of the other, to a spiritual hunger they each had for God that was more important than their differences? They provide an example of how submission transcends differences.

We also divide frequently over *self-wills* that battle to get their way. Yet when we yield our desires to have our way, and balance them with a concern for others ("Do nothing out of selfish ambition or vain conceit, but in humility consider others better than yourselves. Each of you should look not only to your own interests, but also to the interests of others" Philippians 2:3-4), then we can overcome our tendencies to divide and build a practical, Spirit-based unity.

I appreciate one role of the Spirit that particularly allows us to yield to others: "God has poured out his love into our hearts by the Holy Spirit" (Romans 5:5). Submitting to others requires a great amount of godly love for them. God transplants his love for people into us, through the Spirit. So, we can enhance our unity as we lovingly yield to others and resist our own desire to have our way.

INTENTIONALLY TRANSCEND DIVISIONS

Allowing differences to divide us seems like an innate part of our human nature. Peter and Cornelius's experience showed that we can overcome them. But we don't always do that easily. We would prefer to stay in a group of people who are like us. Peter was the same way.

I imagine his spirit soared after seeing what God had done in reaching out to non-Jews. But word of what happened reached home before he did, and attitudes hardened. Charges of "You went into the house of uncircumcised men and ate with them" (Acts 11:3) faced him, and believe me, that was not a compliment. To traditional Jews, Peter's action betrayed his own people.

Peter did two things that we can copy. First, he took a stand. He didn't "wimp out" and back down: "Peter began and explained everything to them precisely as it had happened"

(Acts 11:4). He didn't soften it, and he didn't rationalize it. He didn't try to please people with his answers.

Second, he made it clear that God was behind this event. He simply told what had happened and concluded, "Who was I to think that I could oppose God?" (Act 11:17).

Sometimes we should graciously yield to the opinions of others. But not when God tells us differently. Peter knew this was a "God thing," and he wanted to end up on God's side, on the unity side.

Let me suggest that we should be equally committed to intentionally transcending differences. We have them. We began the chapter looking at some of the differences within Christianity: meta-groups; wings; theological belief systems; religious families; denominations; groups within denominations; groups within local churches; practices, such as contemporary, traditional, or blended worship; Communion being served each week, or month, or quarter.

We must realize that we can lovingly disagree on many things. We just can't allow divisions between different parts of the body of Christ.

BE BOLD

Peter took some courageous steps that went far beyond his comfort zone. When the vision suggested he kill and eat unclean animals, he seemed indignant that God would even suggest such a thing. After all, the Lord should have known Peter better than that! But when Peter realized that unity represented God's will, he gladly went beyond his comfort zone and risked the disapproval of his closest friends in the church.

He went to people different from himself, those with whom he wasn't comfortable, and once he had done so, he stuck with his actions. He changed his life and ministry. He resisted those who resisted transcending differences.

What about us? What areas in our lives have we resisted the call of the Spirit to transcend differences? I would love to list some suggestions here, but I feel much more confident in the

Spirit's ability to know our hearts and to lead us where he desires.

So, take a moment. Ask the Spirit to reveal to you any areas of your life in which you quench him by not being united with other believers, by looking down on them, by separating yourself from them. Then, ask the Spirit to fill you, again, and to lead you into greater unity with other followers of Jesus. Like the old Frank Sinatra song says about love and marriage: you can't have one without the other. Be bold, and "go for both."

Chapter 10

Supernatural Power to Build Intimacy with God

I hadn't been at the church long before Keith asked me *the* question: "Tim, what do you know about the Roswell, New Mexico, incident back in '47? Do you think UFOs exist?" Now, I don't want to get into UFOs here, I really don't, so we won't. Authors have that option. But Keith believed in them, strongly, and wondered how they might fit in with God and the Bible.

Keith represents a lot of people today who look for something beyond the natural and material. Others look in more bizarre regions. Psychics sell their services via the media, we see an ample number of astrology adherents, and many who believe in angels aren't too sure about God. I read some science fiction, and stories abound in which humans meet extraterrestrials that far surpass us terrestrials in intelligence, technology, and values.

Why do we see this happening? Many of us want to gain a sense of transcendence, a sense that something exists that is bigger than we are, something beyond the material stuff of life. What a miserable universe, we conclude, if we are the epitome of it.

But at the same time, we want a transcendence that we can handle. We don't want things too far beyond us. We often view God that way: powerful, but safe; divine, but benign; comforting, but not demanding.

Some seem to think we do God a favor by going to church. Others follow Jesus because "life goes better" that way. We are not drawn to the truth of God, or the joy of knowing the marvelous Creator; the things of life just taste better with a little religion mixed in for flavor. For many of us, God is one factor in our lives, but he certainly doesn't dominate all other concerns.

We have moved away from fearing God to thinking of him as a friend. Let me suggest that two results will occur when we allow the Spirit to fill us. First, we will see how marvelously different God is. We call that "transcendence." Second, we will discover that being filled with the Spirit allows us to connect intimately with this transcendent God.

Comprehend God's Incomprehensibility

Even though God made us in his image, we cannot fully comprehend his nature, being, or attributes. We need to understand that inability of ours and accept it. Transcendence doesn't so much mean that God is just like us only *bigger*, but that he is totally *different* from us. I told Keith that I absolutely believed in extraterrestrials—like God: He wasn't born on this planet. He is not human. He cannot be equated with us, or us with him. So although I prefer not to discuss UFOs, yes, I do believe there are ETs. But not the kind we usually think of when we hear that phrase used by most people.

We can all benefit as we explore just how different God is from us. That sets the stage for how the Spirit brings intimacy with God as he fills us.

TRANSCENDENT BY NATURE

Let's examine some biblical statements that reveal God's transcendence, then I will list others in case you would like to explore this subject further.

Isaiah 55:8-9 may be the classic verses: "'For my thoughts are not your thoughts, neither are your ways my ways,' declares the LORD. 'As the heavens are higher than the earth, so are my ways higher than your ways and my thoughts than your thoughts.'" God himself states that his thoughts and ways far exceed ours. As a result, we can't begin to fully understand the thoughts of God: "Oh, the depth of the riches of the wisdom and knowledge of God! How unsearchable his judgments, and his paths beyond tracing out! 'Who has known the mind of the Lord? Or who has been his counselor?'" (Romans 11:33-34).

I feel just a bit disappointed that God won't choose me as his adviser. But at least he won't choose you either. We just don't measure up.

1 Timothy 6:15-16 increases our perception of the gap between us and "God, the blessed and only Ruler, the King of kings and Lord of lords, who alone is immortal and who lives in *unapproachable light,* whom no one has seen or can see" (emphasis added).

Only God rules the universe. Only God rules over all kings. Only God rules over all lords. Only God is immortal. Most of us have no trouble accepting that truth. But then comes the "kicker": he lives in unapproachable light. In other words, the glory of God is so overwhelming that no human can see him in his fullness and survive to tell about it. When Moses, his faithful servant, asked to see him, God said, "You cannot see my face, for no one may see me and live" (Exodus 33:20).

God hid Moses in a crack in a rock, placed his hand over him, and let him see just a part of his glory as he passed by. From that glimpse, Moses' face glowed so much that the people of Israel couldn't look at him without being blinded (see Exodus 34:29-35). Why did that happen? Because God lives in pure unapproachable light.

The disciples experienced the transcendence of Jesus several times, when he allowed his cloak of humanity to slip away to reveal the deity beneath: "After six days Jesus took with him Peter, James and John the brother of James, and led them up a high mountain by themselves. There he was transfigured before them. *His face shone like the sun, and his clothes became as white as the light"* (Matthew 17:1-2, emphasis added).

While in exile, John the apostle had a similar experience with Jesus:

Among the lampstands was someone "like a son of man," dressed in a robe reaching down to his feet and with a golden sash around his chest. His head and hair were white like wool, as white as snow, and *his eyes were like blazing fire.* His feet were like bronze glowing in a furnace, and his voice was like the sound of rushing waters. In his right hand he held seven stars, and out of his mouth came a sharp double-edged sword. *His face was like the sun shining in all its brilliance.*

When I saw him, I fell at his feet as though dead. Then he placed his right hand on me and said: "Do not be afraid. I am the First and the Last. I am the Living One; I was dead, and behold I am alive for ever and ever!" (Revelation 1:13–18, emphasis added).

Just a glimpse of deity tends to overwhelm us, doesn't it? The way we are "wired," we just can't handle the fullness of God. It is kind of like running 220 volts of electricity through a 12-volt system. The inevitable result is overload.

(If you would like to explore this subject more fully, take a look at these passages: 1 Kings 8:10–11; Exodus 24:15–17; Exodus 33–34; Isaiah 6:1–7; Job 38–41; Mark 4: 35–41; Revelation 1:9–19. If you have a Bible search program, try entering "glory" and "Lord" and explore those passages also.)

TRANSCENDENT BY HOLINESS

God's very nature exceeds ours and results in our inability to approach him. But the difference in our behavior has the same result. We call that difference holiness. He has it, we don't. And that difference makes a *big* difference.

Just for fun, I punched "holy" and "lord" into my computer Bible program, and 193 verses popped up. Even the "intellectually challenged" like me can see quite a connection between these two terms.

Isaiah 6:1–3 emphasizes that holiness permeates God, that it defines him:

> In the year that King Uzziah died, I saw the Lord seated on a throne, high and exalted, and the train of his robe filled the temple. Above him were seraphs, each with six wings: With two wings they covered their faces, with two they covered their feet, and with two they were flying. And they were calling to one another: *"Holy, holy, holy is the LORD Almighty; the whole earth is full of his glory"* (emphasis added).

Instead of using bold or italics for emphasis, as we do today, in biblical times writers used repetition. Repeating something once meant that it was important. Repeating it again gave it maximum emphasis. In this passage, the angels cried "holy" three times to describe God. That absolute purity of character and behavior flows from his very nature and identity.

For us to relate to God, we need to be on a level playing field with him, we need to share his primary character trait, according to Hebrews 12:14: "Make every effort to live in peace with all men and to be holy; *without holiness no one will see the Lord"* (emphasis added).

Here we come to "the rock and the hard place" we discussed earlier: God is holy. We need to be holy to see him. But, we don't even come close to being holy, and that lack of holiness on our part builds a wall of separation between us and him: "But there is a problem—*your sins have cut you off from God.* Because of your sin, he has turned away and will not listen anymore" (Isaiah 59:2 NLT, emphasis added).

To summarize these verses, God's holiness transcends ours. As much as we might yearn to know God and come close to him, we cannot bridge that gap between us. By nature and by holiness, he is far removed from us. We must comprehend God's incomprehensibility. We must realize that because of the difference between us, he is totally unapproachable to us. But how does all this fit into being filled with the Spirit? The Spirit helps us overcome that insurmountable difference.

Transcend Transcendence

Here, we will examine some of the ways that the Spirit brings us closer to the Father. Basically, the more we allow the Spirit to fill our lives, the more he can work in us, the closer to his character we become, and the more intimacy we have with God.

Know that God desires intimacy with us. He sent his Son to take on all of our sin in order to allow us that intimacy with him. The Old Testament provides the best description of the relationship God yearns to have with us:

> "This is the covenant I will make with the house of Israel after that time," declares the LORD. "I will put my law in their minds and write it on their hearts. I will be their God, and they will be my people.
>
> "No longer will a man teach his neighbor, or a man his brother, saying, 'Know the LORD,' because they will all know me, from the least of them to the greatest," declares the LORD.
>
> "For I will forgive their wickedness and will remember their sins no more" (Jeremiah 31:33-34).

Remember, holiness plays a crucial role in achieving this intimacy with God, and Jesus begins that process: "We have *been made holy* through the sacrifice of the body of Jesus Christ once for all" (Hebrews 10:10, emphasis added). That verse is in the past tense. We are already holy. The job is finished. Or is it?

Not quite. Or rather, yes and no. God *views* us as holy, but we are still in the *process* of becoming more holy in practice. Let's move just a few verses later to Hebrews 10:14: "By one sacrifice he has made perfect forever those who are *being made holy*" (emphasis added). Verse 10 said we have *been* made holy, verse 14 says we are *being* made holy. Which is it? Have we been made holy or are we being made holy? The answer is "both."

When we come to Jesus, he wraps his arms around us, covers us with his holiness, and God sees that holiness when he looks at us. The barrier of unrighteousness has been removed so that God now sees us as holy. But we don't always live that holiness. Jesus started the job, and the Spirit finishes it. Let's explore how he does that.

A BIG GOD IN A LITTLE BOX

Think about the utter transcendence of God. Think about the immeasurable gap between us. Think about the total intimacy that God desires between us. Now, ponder what happens when the Spirit lives in us. First, God provides the Spirit as a guarantee that he will fulfill his promise to help us become more holy.

"[God] put his Spirit in our hearts as a *deposit*, guaranteeing what is to come" (2 Corinthians 1:22, emphasis added). That word "deposit" in this verse refers to a real estate transaction; we use it in the same way today. We see a house we want to buy, make an offer on it, and give some money to the agent to hold for us. That money is called a deposit. We lose that deposit if we don't follow through on the contract. If God doesn't follow through on his promise to help us become more holy, then he will forfeit his deposit, which is the Spirit, or, a part of himself. So God has put a lot on the line to offer us intimacy.

The presence of the Spirit within us reminds us of just how much God cherishes intimacy with us. But that presence accomplishes one more task, one that amazes me. The Spirit brings the actual, direct presence of the transcendent God into us.

Jesus told us, "And I will ask the Father, and he will give you another Counselor to be with you forever—the Spirit of truth. The world cannot accept him, because it neither sees him nor knows him. But you know him, *for he lives with you and will be in you*" (John 14:16-17, emphasis added).

Since the Father and the Spirit are one, when the Spirit comes into our lives, God comes into our lives—the God whom we otherwise couldn't know without holiness. Now, how does an eternal, omniscient, omnipotent being live within us? I don't have a clue how a powerful God fits himself into a puny human.

When I was just a kid, I awoke one Christmas morning to find a *huge* package under the tree, with my name on it. This had to be the biggest and best Christmas gift of all time, I thought, and it was mine! So I tore the wrapping paper off, and found another package, just slightly smaller. Hmm. This was something new to me. I tore that paper off, and found another box. I went through six boxes before getting to the gift. Honestly, I can't remember the gift, only how disappointed I was.

God does just the opposite here in this situation. We are the tiny package, with a *huge* gift inside—God himself. So becoming a Christian doesn't just mean that our sins are forgiven, or that we accept new values, that we pursue God, that we change our lifestyle. All of these wonderful things should occur. But the most astounding change of all is that God lives in us, through the Spirit. And, that Spirit wants to fill every nook and cranny of our lives with God.

REFINER'S FIRE

But it gets even better. We have been made holy, but we still need more work to develop our maximum intimacy with God. Earlier in John 14, Jesus promised us that the Spirit would live in us. That indwelling presence of the Spirit allows the next step toward holiness, as Jesus described in verse 26: "But the Counselor, the Holy Spirit, whom the Father will send in my name, will *teach you all things* and will remind you of everything I have said to you" (emphasis added).

How do we become more holy? By the Spirit teaching us, convicting us, correcting us, and empowering us. Since he lives within us, he knows all our secrets, our rationalizations, our weaknesses, our excuses. And he knows which of these things we don't even know about ourselves. I have some of those unknowns in my life, just as you do in your life.

As a teenager and college student, I "burned the candle at both ends" quite frequently. Late nights working with the college group at one church required even more catching up on sleep, and I loved to sleep late. Grabbing an extra half hour felt like winning the lottery without buying a ticket. I just can't relate to people who get up early at the same time each morning because their body won't let them sleep in.

But one morning in the early days of our marriage, I lay in bed as Sheila kissed me goodbye on her way to work. Suddenly I felt a twinge inside. Could I be allowing too much room for laziness in my life? I didn't realize it then, but looking back, the Spirit did some teaching that morning. So, since then, I set the alarm as a part of regular daily routine. I do so because I want to build more self-discipline in my life.

Have you experienced that same kind of twinge? An act that felt fine for years suddenly becomes something you feel guilty about. So, you change. You become more holy. That twinge may touch on relatively insignificant areas like sleeping in too late, or it may touch on major areas of sin in your life. But with the Spirit living within us and knowing us so well, he can easily teach us how to become holier. He can refine us—sometimes by fire; sometimes by a small whisper.

But I encourage you to listen carefully to those nudges. Much of the time, they are signs that the Spirit is trying to get your attention and move you further along the holiness road.

Glory Giver

The late Bob Hope once took a new comedienne, Phyllis Diller, on one of his tours to entertain American troops in Vietnam, and her material flopped. It just didn't work for that audience. After Hope's recent death, Diller told how Hope got his writers to develop a new act for her. But to Diller's surprise, Hope played the straight man; she had all the gag lines. She was astounded that such an established celebrity possessed enough humility to give away the "good stuff."

The Spirit works like that in us. He wants us to look good. He wants us to have holiness. And the more we allow him to fill us, the more room we make within us for holiness. But how can that be? Here's how it works:

In a passage that begins much like one we examined earlier, Jesus said:

> "I have much more to say to you, more than you can now bear. But when he, the Spirit of truth, comes, he will guide you into all truth. He will not speak on his own; he will speak only what he hears, and he will tell you what is yet to come. He will bring glory to me by *taking from what is mine and making it known to you.* All that belongs to the Father is mine. That is why I said the Spirit will take from what is mine and make it known to you" (John 16:12-15, emphasis added).

Based on what we have seen, what belongs to both the Father and the Son? Glory, holiness, purity. The Spirit within us allows us to experience the glory of God personally and directly.

Have you ever had a habit that you just couldn't overcome? Then you felt that twinge that told you it was wrong, and you asked God for some extra power to deal with it. That power brought a success that you couldn't achieve on your own. When that happened to you, what did you feel? A small touch of the glory of God.

The more we are filled, the more glory we experience. Then we are drawn to God even more as we see his value. As we become more intimate with him, the Spirit plays a greater role in our lives, and we experience *more* of God's glory. So we become addicted to it, and want even more of it. That is a nice process, isn't it? And it all begins with letting the Spirit fill us. But not only can we *see* and *experience* God's glory, the Spirit helps us to possess it.

Let's go back to a passage we have quoted often, 2 Corinthians 3:18: "And all of us, with unveiled faces, seeing the glory of the Lord as though reflected in a mirror, are being transformed into the same image *from one degree of glory to another;* for *this comes from* the Lord, *the Spirit*" (NRSV, emphasis added).

Not only do we *see* the Lord's glory, not only do we *experience* God's glory, but the Spirit *transforms* us into that glory, one step at a time. Each time we listen to the Spirit convicting us of a sin and change, we receive a little more of God's glory. Each time we say yes when he leads us into a ministry, we receive a little more of God's glory. Each time we act in love toward someone who is unlovely, we receive a little more of God's glory. Each time we forgive a wrong, we receive a little more of God's glory.

Through the filling of the Holy Spirit, all of the obstacles of sin that hinder our intimacy with God are removed. We come closer *to* God, and in so doing, we become more *like* God. But all of that happens only when we continue in that process of being filled with the Spirit *of* God.

Chapter 11

Supernatural Power to Get Through Life

Cam provided a great picture of his spiritual life: "I saw the Christian journey like a cruise—relaxing, luxurious, with a marvelous cruise director. I expected that this cruise would avoid the storms of the sea. So when some storms came up, I talked to the cruise director, who suggested I read the cruise brochure. Boy, was I surprised! It did mention them. But even then, I didn't expect all the bumps that came along."

Karen picked up the story, "When I became pregnant with our first child, tests revealed I had a malignant tumor on an ovary. So my pregnancy saved my life, but I needed a hysterectomy, and the chemo treatments just wiped me out. I'm still feeling their effects."

Cam interrupted, "Don't begin to think we haven't battled about this. It has affected our marriage and our faith; it has not been an easy 'cruise.' But God has been with us, each step of the way. Without him, I don't know how we would have made it through."

Have you seen that popular bumper sticker, "Life is tough; then you die"? On our spiritual journey, we face an abundance of difficulties, problems, decisions, questions, and bumps in the road. But when we allow the Spirit to fill us, he guides us through the maze of life.

In this final chapter, we will put together many of the concepts we have previously discussed to see how they relate to our journey through life. When we choose to follow Jesus, we don't just choose to receive the Spirit; we don't just choose to be filled. Rather, we choose the life of the Spirit, which is a paradigm shift in the way we view our spiritual journey. The life of the Spirit allows us to cooperate with all that he wants to accomplish in our lives.

Life Happens

A maze confronts us with an abundance of choices. However, we can't see where each choice leads, and so confusion grows. Do we turn to the left, or the right, or just keep going straight ahead? What comes next? At times I have said to God, "Father, I'll go anywhere you want me to go and do anything you want me to do, just tell me what you want!" I get frustrated when I look at the options and obstacles in life. They abound in my life, and probably in yours as well. Let's look at some of them.

Typical Troubles

Cam discovered the promise Jesus gave in John 16:33: "Here on earth you will have many trials and sorrows" (NLT). So far, I haven't found that particular promise in any of the books that describe the wonderful promises Jesus has made to us. We expect an easy cruise, but life gives us an abundance of difficulties. Health, financial, relational, and spiritual obstacles are *normal*, not exceptional. And each of these presents us with difficulties as we attempt to make our way through the maze of life.

Bad Advisers

Several years ago, Sheila and I had a little bit of money to put into an IRA, so we looked around carefully for a good place to invest it. A friend had just started working with an investment firm, and his supervisor recommended an oil investment, which he in turn recommended to us. We thought we couldn't lose: if gas prices went up, our investment would prosper; if gas prices went down, our monthly budget would prosper.

Somehow, gas prices went up even as our oil investment went down. We never used that investment company again.

Spiritually, bad advisers can present obstacles in our spiritual life as well as in our natural life. In Matthew 23:1–33 Jesus criticized some of the spiritual leaders of his day. Five times he called them blind, and seven times he called them hypocrites. Look how he vividly described their ministry: "Woe to you, teachers of the law and Pharisees, you hypocrites! You travel over land and sea to win a single convert, and when he becomes one, you make him twice as much a son of hell as you are" (Matthew 23:15).

Bad spiritual advice, whether from a book, a sermon, or a conversation, can add to the confusion of life.

PATHETIC PRAYER

Probably nothing builds intimacy with God or provides direction through life as effectively as prayer. So when we struggle in prayer, we lose both of those benefits. Most of us feel inadequate in our prayers, which is nothing new. The early disciples felt discouraged about their praying too, as we see in Luke 11:1: "One day Jesus was praying in a certain place. When he finished, one of his disciples said to him, 'Lord, teach us to pray, just as John taught his disciples.'"

Apparently, the early church didn't fully learn that lesson, which Paul expressed in Romans 8:26: "We do not know how to pray as we should" (NASB). So when our prayers are pathetic, we lose a significant ability to work our way through the maze of life.

LIMITED PERCEPTIONS

Since high school, I have needed glasses for distance vision. I couldn't stand wearing them full time, so I stuck a pair in my pocket on the way to class. And I kept a pair in my car as standard equipment. I tried contact lenses, and they helped, but wearing them full time just didn't work. So a few years ago I had laser eye surgery, and it went fairly well. Afterwards, I had about 20/40 vision, and could see pretty clearly, so I gave away my glasses.

But my vision wasn't as crisp as the doctor desired, so I had an enhancement. Recently I went in for a checkup, and I now have 20/15 vision. I can see so clearly that details just jump out at me. I can't wait to travel to the Sierras to see all the stars in their glory.

When we can't see clearly, we can't easily determine where to go. In the maze analogy, the hedge that surrounds us doesn't extend upward to infinity, just high enough to keep us from peeping over it. Spiritually, we have limited vision.

> For we know in part and we prophesy in part, but when perfection comes, the imperfect disappears. When I was a child, I talked like a child, I thought like a child, I reasoned like a child. When I became a man, I put childish ways behind me. *Now we see but a poor reflection as in a mirror;* then we shall see face to face. Now I know in part; then I shall know fully, even as I am fully known (1 Corinthians 13:9–12, emphasis added).

We just don't see all the reality that exists. We don't usually see angels, unless we watch reruns of the television series *Touched by an Angel.* We don't usually see demons, unless we watch some rock bands. We don't see all the dimensions of life, so we find it hard to navigate through the maze of life. As a result, life gets confusing. We don't always know the right direction to take; we don't always know how to handle the problems that arise. We need help.

Choose the Spirit

I am convinced that rather than life being a maze with hundreds of choices, we truly face only three.

The *unspiritual life* has no significant contact with God. The person choosing this life works through the maze of life by personal wisdom, preferences, and strength. The apostle Paul described this journey in 1 Corinthians 2:14: "The man *without the Spirit* does not accept the things that come from the Spirit of God, for they are foolishness to him, and *he cannot understand them*, because they are spiritually discerned" (emphasis added). I followed that path for several years, as do many people, and found that although we do get through life, we miss out on spiritual resources that would help us get through the maze.

The *worldly Christian life* has a connection to Christ, but limits God's ability to work. In the context of this book, we would call these these non–Spirit-filled believers, which Paul described a few verses later. He clearly talked to Christian brothers, but ones who hadn't plunged into the fullness of the Spirit:

> Brothers, I could not address you as spiritual but as *worldly—mere infants in Christ*. I gave you milk, not solid food, for you were not yet ready for it. Indeed, you are still not ready. *You are still worldly.* For since there is jealousy and quarreling among you, are you not worldly? Are you not acting like mere men? (1 Corinthians 3:1–3, emphasis added).

Such believers reach out to God with one hand, and hold onto worldly ways with the other, thus preventing the Spirit from filling, guiding, and empowering them. They have more spiritual resources to deal with the maze of life than unspiritual people, but they don't use all that is available to them. They accurately feel torn in two directions.

The *spiritual life* provides all we have talked about so far, as tools we can use to successfully work through the maze. But even so, let's refine the choices. We truly choose one of two directions—toward sin or toward God. Jesus prefers that we definitively choose one or the other, if for no other reason than to be very clear about the direction of our lives. He spoke to a group of Christians at the church in Laodicea and said: "I know your deeds, that you are neither cold nor hot. I wish you were either one or the other! *So, because you are lukewarm—neither hot nor cold—I am about to spit you out of my mouth"* (Revelation 3:15–16, emphasis added).

God wants us to choose our direction, and to pursue it. In Galatians 5:16-17 Paul expressed these two mutually exclusive options: "So I say, live by the Spirit, and you will not gratify the desires of the sinful nature. For the sinful nature desires what is contrary to the Spirit, and the Spirit what is contrary to the sinful nature. They are in conflict with each other, so that you do not do what you want."

We have two options: we gratify our sinful desires, and suffer the consequences of such an unspiritual life, or we craft our lives so that the Spirit can fill us, and we can live each moment in step with him. It is our choice. Each way has consequences, but God lets us choose which path we will follow. Let's look at what it means to choose the Spirit rather than the flesh.

JUST SAY NO TO SIN

Back in Galatians 5:16-17, Paul clearly said that we need to reject our sinful desires if we want to choose the life of the Spirit. We all begin with a bent toward sin. Coming to Christ means that we choose a life of holiness instead of continuing in the direction of sin. Let's look at signs of a life that stays stuck in sin:

> The acts of the sinful nature are obvious: sexual immorality, impurity and debauchery; idolatry and witchcraft; hatred, discord, jealousy, fits of rage, selfish ambition, dissensions, factions and envy; drunkenness, orgies, and the like. I warn you, as I did before, that those who live like this will not inherit the kingdom of God (Galatians 5:19-21).

So, we choose these acts, or we choose the Spirit. Does that mean that Christians will *never* do any of these things? Wouldn't that be nice? But we recognize that kind of wishful thinking doesn't match reality. Christians will still sin, the New Testament makes that point clear: "If we claim to be without sin, we deceive ourselves and the truth is not in us" (1 John 1:8). But the *direction* of our lives should be away from these sinful things. The deepest desire of our heart should be to avoid them. Yes, we have a desire to sin; otherwise we wouldn't do it. And it does bring pleasure; otherwise we wouldn't engage in it.

These acts of the sinful nature seem to fit into four basic categories, which may help us grasp the concept more easily. The *New International Version* even divides them this way, with a semi-colon between the groupings:

Moral Purity: "sexual immorality, impurity and debauchery." When the Spirit fills us, he leads us away from any type of sexual sin. So if we want to know how to get through the moral dilemmas of life, we avoid these negative things.

Spiritual Purity: "idolatry and witchcraft." When the Spirit fills us, we don't look anywhere else for supernatural advice or strength, meaning that we don't dabble in things like ouija boards, tarot, astrology, and trance channeling. So if we want direction to get through the maze of life, we avoid these negative things.

Relationship Purity: "hatred, discord, jealousy, fits of rage, selfish ambition, dissensions, factions and envy." All of us value relationships. Recent studies show that when we have better relationships, we have better health. So if we want help in getting through relationship difficulties, we stay away from these negative things.

Self-Control: "drunkenness, orgies, and the like." If we don't exercise self-control in every area of our life, we can get pulled away from God. So as we make decisions about how to navigate the maze of life, we must learn to say no to ourselves. We must stay away from these negative things.

Did you notice the result Paul indicated if we allow these acts to dominate our lives? He said that we will not inherit the kingdom of God. Why? Because we have chosen to ignore the life of holiness, the life of the Spirit, the life of God. This type of behavior makes it clear that we don't desire the godly life. If we don't desire the godly life, then we don't desire God. Remember, we can't separate the two. But when we choose the Spirit, then we can resist our sinful nature and gain the victory over sinful acts.

LIVE WITH THE SPIRIT

In Galatians 5:16-17 Paul clarified the two basic options that face us: choosing to follow our sinful nature, or choosing to follow the Spirit. In verses 19-21 he described the former. In verses 22-24 he describes what it means to be led by the Spirit:

> But the fruit of the Spirit is love, joy, peace, patience, kindness, goodness, faithfulness, gentleness and self-control. Against such things there is no law. Those who belong to Christ Jesus have crucified the sinful nature with its passions and desires.

That last sentence emphasizes our need to make a clean break of direction. Even though sin will always influence us, we need to make a decisive choice to move with the Spirit. Remember, God yearns for progressive victory, but that victory begins with putting an end to the reign of sin in our lives.

So, we work through the maze of life by evaluating each option: does this move me closer to sin, or closer to the Spirit? I have found that facing each situation with that thought in mind really helps me see the situation more clearly. The majority of us don't struggle the most in *knowing* whether something represents sin or the Spirit, we struggle most in *choosing and following* the way of the Spirit. Mark Twain knew that dilemma well: "It's not the things in the Bible that I don't understand that bother me. What bothers me is what I understand and don't do."

In my first book I explored how each facet of the fruit of the Spirit represents a character trait of God. The more intimacy we build with him, and the more we nurture his traits, the more godly we become. Each of these facets of the fruit of the Spirit will guide us internally through the maze of life.

Here's what I mean. When these character traits grow in our lives, then we evaluate options on the basis of what best builds and expresses that character:

What option best expresses *love?* How can I best act in the spiritual interest of other people? Am I motivated by selfish interest, or do I truly care for them?

What option best expresses *joy?* Am I driven by happiness, which flows from what happens to me at the moment, or do I have deep-seated and abiding joy over the presence of God in my life?

What option best expresses *peace?* Which option will cause me to strive and worry? Which will lead to a tranquil spirit that trusts in God?

What option best expresses *patience?* Do I quit when troubles come to me, or do I hang in there and see what God desires to do with the difficulties?

What option best expresses *kindness?* How can I best express a tender heart and loving concern? How can I avoid harshness?

What option best expresses *goodness?* Do I have an innate desire to do what is good, or to do what is expedient? Do I try to get as close as possible to the edge of the cliff of wrong without quite stepping over it, or do I stay well away from any hint of wrong?

What option best expresses *faithfulness?* Do I stick with commitments even when they prove difficult or costly? Or do I squirm out when I see something better come along?

What option best expresses *gentleness?* Can I respond to a problem with control rather than losing my temper? Can I act to meet the needs of the other person rather than reacting in my weakness?

What option best expresses *self-control?* Which option represents the easiest alternative; which represents the best alternative? Can I say no to my desires in order to move closer to what the Spirit yearns for me?

When the Spirit lives in us and fills us, these traits become part of our nature. They replace the old sinful nature. They give us direction when we face the maze of life.

I used to yearn for God to speak in an audible voice, telling me exactly what to do. I would have been glad to do it, if only he had spoken to me and told me what to do. But I don't think he works that way. He gives us something better than an audible voice—through his Spirit, he lives in us, he fills us, and he gives us his character.

That character guides us through the problems of life, the pain, the difficulties, the confusion, the uncertainty—each step of each day.

A Final Word of Encouragement

Are you ready to live supernaturally? Are you ready to step into the great adventure of the Spirit? Read this encouragement written by a good friend and sometimes co-author, David Timms. David serves as head of the Graduate Ministries Department at Hope International University. He sent out this message in his *In HOPE* newsletter on August 8, 2003:

> Some of us couldn't sustain a cactus in the crusty conditions we call our lives. Here's a prayer for any of us who know this experience. Perhaps you'd like to take 3–5 minutes and pray this—not just read it.
>
> Holy Spirit, rain on me. The soil of my life is dry and thirsty. I need the refreshing and nourishing touch that only you can bring. But please, go easy. Be gentle.
>
> Do not come as a sprinkling shower. The light mist fails to penetrate. It tantalizes and promises but barely penetrates the surface. My heart is far too dry for that. A light shower will not close the cracks that have opened up. My self-reliance has produced fissures that need more than a few passing droplets.
>
> Do not come as a deluge. I want so much of you, but my heart resists you like a baked tile. To be overwhelmed by your flooding Presence simply

leaves me ... well, overwhelmed for a moment. Then I find that little has changed. The hard crust has formed with time and may take time to loosen.

Do not come as seasonal condensation. I need you as much in the chilly winters of non-productivity, the breezy autumns of change, and the scorching summers of conflict, as in the pleasant spring seasons when all seems well. The soil of my heart, the garden of my soul, needs your steady Presence. Come again, and again ... and abide.

Come as a soaking Presence. Let me drink of you not in gulps but sips. Let my barrenness and dryness be transformed so that roses flower in this desert. Soak steadily. Soak deeply. And as the top layers rejuvenate, continue to course deeper and deeper within me, softening the clay, infiltrating the buried layers that I hide, seeping into the deepest aquifers.

Spirit of God, come. Come beside me. Come upon me. Come within me. But come. Come gently. Come surely. Bring your replenishing Presence into my life.

Are you ready to pray that kind of earnest, heartfelt prayer? Does it represent the deepest yearning of your heart? Then allow the Spirit to fill you, as we have talked about, and you will receive the promise of Galatians 5:25: *Since we live by the Spirit, let us keep in step with the Spirit.*

Readers' Guide

CHAPTER ONE

1   What happens when we choose to walk where the Spirit leads us?

2   How does being filled with the Spirit affect our desire for God? Our desire to open the "secret junk rooms" hidden in our lives?

3   When, according to Acts 2:38, does the process of being filled begin?

4   Why is it important for us to recognize that the Holy Spirit is fully God (Colossians 2:9) and yet possesses the qualities of a person?

5   What stood out as you read about biblical characters who were filled with the Spirit?

6   What happens if we try to live victorious Christian lives without being filled with the Spirit?

7   According to the author, what is the relationship between *being filled with the Spirit* and the *baptism of the Spirit*?

CHAPTER TWO

1 In what ways do we put out the Spirit's fire? (See 1 Thessalonians 5:19.) Conversely, what can we do to allow "the fire" of the Spirit to burn within us?

2 Why do you think the Spirit will not do his purifying work within us without our permission? (See Luke 11:9-13.)

3 What is holiness? What's the relationship between being filled with the *Holy* Spirit and our desire for holiness?

4 What are the five steps we must take in order to carry out the one command to be filled? (See Ephesians 5:18-21 KJV.) Which one(s) do you think are easier, and which are harder? Why? What are some reasons why we resist doing these?

5 What does it mean, in practical terms, to "live by the Spirit" daily? (See Galatians 5:16, 25.)

CHAPTER THREE

1 Why do we so often attempt to meet challenges in our own strength instead of in the Spirit's power?

2 What happens in our lives when we don't recognize the Spirit's power?

3   Jesus' ministry depended on the Spirit's power. (See Luke 4:14.) How might our lives (and our ministry) be different if we relied on the Spirit's power to transform our lives?

4   Which tasks in your life create fear? What did you think about when you read, "God doesn't just give us a task we fear, he also provides the power we need to succeed in it, through the Spirit"?

Chapter Four

1   What kinds of things keep us "stuck in the pot" (like the author's camellia plant) and limit our spiritual growth?

2   What are some reasons why we don't choose to allow the Spirit to fill us and consequently limit our spiritual growth?

3   What does it mean to be "transformed" into the likeness of Jesus? (See 2 Corinthians 3:17-18.)

4   Do you believe that a Christian can regain the ability to accurately express God's likeness? Why or why not? How might our answers to this question influence our attitudes toward spiritual growth?

5   How can we, through the Spirit, discover the plans God has for us? What does it mean to have "the mind of Christ"? Why is this such an important principle to understand?

6   In what way(s) can our clinging to the "good" be the most effective enemy of the "best" God has for us? What are some examples of this?

CHAPTER FIVE

1   What can happen when we spend more time learning the Bible than we do telling non-Christians about Jesus, demonstrating his love, and serving them?

2   According to 1 Peter 3:15,
    What should we focus on when we tell others about Jesus?

    Why it is important for us to be able to answer questions about what God has done, and is doing, in our lives?

3   Why don't many Christians have non-Christians friends? What kinds of meaningful contact do you have with non-Christians? What might you do this coming week to get to know a non-Christian neighbor or friend better?

4   Why do Christians tend to associate the filling of the Spirit with the charismatic gifts? How has what you read in this chapter influenced your beliefs about the filling of the Spirit?

5   As revealed in such New Testament passages as Acts 4—7, what was the relationship between being filled with the Spirit and the courage, faith, and ministry impact of the early Christians? How does this truth relate to us today, particularly our impact as witnesses for Jesus?

CHAPTER SIX

1   Discussing Matthew 10:39, the author stated that if we enhance our individuality for ourselves, we won't achieve our full potential. What do we do to enhance our individuality for ourselves? Why do we do these things?

2   What have you done to cultivate your unique blend of natural abilities? Which spiritual gift(s) do you think the Holy Spirit has given you? (See 1 Corinthians 12:7–11, 28; Romans 12:6–8; Ephesians 4:11; 1 Peter 4:10–11.) Remember, we each learn our gift(s) by serving.

3   Why does the Spirit give us spiritual gifts? (See 1 Corinthians 12:7.)

4   Even if we don't yet know our individual, God-given gift(s), why is it important for each of us to *use* our God-given gifts—to serve, to minister, to try different tasks and arenas—to see which one(s) God and other people seem to confirm?

5   The author wrote, "Gifts come from the Spirit, the specific arena of ministry comes from Jesus, and the results come from the Father." Why is it important for us to remember that the Father provides the results that flow from our use of the gifts?

6   Which difficult task(s) beyond your abilities may God want you to try so you can see what God can do in you?

CHAPTER SEVEN

1   What is the relationship between being filled with the Spirit and our willingness to embrace and live by the "full" truth?

2   What kinds of things do we do to "resist truth" and therefore make it impossible for the Spirit to fill us?

3   Do you agree or disagree with this statement: "We need to listen to those who speak the truth to us about our lives"? Why or why not? What happens when we ignore the truth about ourselves? About our sins? About temptations? About our gifts and abilities?

4   Do you agree that our choices *show* whether or not we really want intimacy with the Spirit or the alternatives? Why or why not?

5   What does it mean to "speak truth" to one another? How can we do this "in love"? (See Ephesians 4:15, 26–27, 29–32.)

6   What did you think about when you read Psalm 51:1–5? How do these verses apply to being Spirit led and building a life of integrity that pleases the Spirit?

CHAPTER EIGHT

1   Do you find it easy or difficult to treasure what God treasures, to gain your significance from what you have stored

up in heaven? Why? Why is it so hard to not build a world around living for ourselves?

2   What do 1 Timothy 6:17-19 and 1 Corinthians 3:10-15 reveal about the spiritual legacy we can build up for ourselves in heaven?

3   What do some Christians resist ministering to other people? What do these Christians miss as a result? (See Ephesians 4:13-14.)

4   Why do our motives play such a crucial role in whether or not the ministry we do results in "treasure in heaven"?

5   Do you believe "when God leads us, we can attempt the impossible," which often results in something wonderful? Why or why not? What does your answer reveal about your willingness to rely on the Spirit and faithfully do the ministry God has given you?

6   What impact does our character have on our ministry effectiveness? What role does the Spirit play in crafting a new character for each of us? (See 2 Corinthians 3:18.)

CHAPTER NINE

1   As you read the verses on unity in this chapter, what did you think about? What is the link between the Spirit—who fills, leads, and empowers us—and our complete unity? (See John 17:23 and Ephesians 4:3.)

2   What are some practical ways in which we can develop Spirit-led unity in order to reach the world for Christ?

3   How should we respond to disunity, in light of the verses in this chapter? Which attitudes will we have to face in ourselves when we do this?

4   What practical things can we Christians do to preserve the unity of the Spirit we already have so it doesn't decrease? What does "loving disagreement" look like, practically speaking, and what keeps it from becoming divisions between different parts of the body of Christ?

5   What does it mean to submit to other Christians? Why is submission a requirement in building complete unity with others? How does submission relate to our need sometimes to take firm stands for what God reveals?

6   In which area(s) of your life have you quenched the Spirit by resisting his call to transcend differences and be fully united with other believers? If you haven't already done so, which steps will you take to be filled again by the Spirit and establish greater, full unity with other followers of Jesus?

CHAPTER TEN

1   Why is it important for us to understand how different God is from us and that we can't fully comprehend his nature?

2   How does the Spirit's filling bring us closer to the Father?

3   What role does our holiness play in achieving intimacy with God? How can we say that we have been made holy and that we are also being made holy?

4   How did you feel when you read that God, through the Spirit, lives in you and wants to "fill every nook and cranny" of your life with himself? And that he, who knows all your secrets, wants to teach you how to become more holy? Why?

5   "The more we are filled," wrote the author, "the more [of God's] glory we experience. Then we are drawn to God even more as we see his value. As we become more intimate with him, the Spirit plays a greater role in our lives, and we experience more of God's glory." What keeps some Christians from desiring this process in their lives?

CHAPTER ELEVEN
1   What are the differences between the *unspiritual life*, the *worldly Christian life*, and the *spiritual life*?

2   Read Galatians 5:16-17, 19-21. According to verses 16-17, what are the two, mutually exclusive options we can choose? What are some signs of a sinful life? (See verses 19-21.)

3   What does it mean, in practical terms, to reject our sinful desires and choose the life of the Spirit—a direction away from sinful things?

4   How would our lives be different if we each asked ourselves this question when making choices: "Does this move me closer to sin, or closer to the Spirit?"

5   Each facet of the fruit of the Spirit mentioned in Galatians 5:22-24 represents a character trait of God. When the Spirit lives in us and fills us, we develop more intimacy with God and nurture his traits, which become part of our nature. Read each of these traits aloud, then discuss how the Spirit uses the character of God to guide us as we make decisions.

6   Reread the prayer at the end of this chapter. Then take time to review what you've learned from this book and how, with the Spirit's help, you will apply these truths in daily life.

The Word at Work Around the World

A vital part of Cook Communications Ministries is our international outreach, Cook Communications Ministries International (CCMI). Your purchase of this book, and of other books and Christian-growth products from Cook, enables CCMI to provide Bibles and Christian literature to people in more than 150 languages in 65 countries.

Cook Communications Ministries is a not-for-profit, self-supporting organization. Revenues from sales of our books, Bible curricula, and other church and home products not only fund our U.S. ministry, but also fund our CCMI ministry around the world. One hundred percent of donations to CCMI go to our international literature programs.

CCMI reaches out internationally in three ways:

· Our premier International Christian Publishing Institute (ICPI) trains leaders from nationally led publishing houses around the world.

· We provide literature for pastors, evangelists, and Christian workers in their national language.

· We reach people at risk—refugees, AIDS victims, street children, and famine victims—with God's Word.

Word Power, God's Power

Faith Kidz, RiverOak, Honor, Life Journey, Victor, NexGen — every time you purchase a book produced by Cook Communications Ministries, you not only meet a vital personal need in your life or in the life of someone you love, but you're also a part of ministering to José in Colombia, Humberto in Chile, Gousa in India, or Lidiane in Brazil. You help make it possible for a pastor in China, a child in Peru, or a mother in West Africa to enjoy a life-changing book. And because you helped, children and adults around the world are learning God's Word and walking in his ways.

Thank you for your partnership in helping to disciple the world. May God bless you with the power of his Word in your life.

For more information about our international ministries, visit www.ccmi.org.

Additional copies of
TWELVE LIES YOU HEAR ABOUT THE HOLY SPIRIT
and other NexGen titles
are available from your local bookseller.

✠ ✠ ✠

If you have enjoyed this book,
or if it has had an impact on your life,
we would like to hear from you.

Please contact us at:

NexGen
Cook Communications Ministries, Dept. 201
4050 Lee Vance View
Colorado Springs, CO 80918
Or at our website: www.cookministries.com